MW00627392

Fathering
from the
Fast Lane

Practical ideas
for busy dads

Bruce Robinson

FINCH PUBLISHING
SYDNEY

This book is dedicated to Chris Beale and Tony Weller, two men whose commitment to fathering helped inspire this book and who died during its preparation. Their contribution to the book extends beyond words.

Bruce Robinson

Fathering from the Fast Lane: Practical ideas for busy dads
This edition first published in 2001 in Australia and New Zealand by Finch Publishing Pty Limited, ABN 49 057 285 248, P O Box 120, Lane Cove, NSW 1595, Australia.

08 07 06 8 7 6 5 4

The National Library of Australia Cataloguing-in-Publication entry:

> Robinson, Bruce W. S.
> Fathering from the fast lane: practical ideas for busy dads.
>
> Bibliography.
> Includes index.
> ISBN 1 876451 21 1.
>
> 1. Fathers - Australia - Interviews. 2. Fatherhood -
> Australia. 3. Father and child - Australia. 4. Work and
> family - Australia. I. Title.
>
> 306.8742

Edited by Sarah Shrubb
Text designed and typeset in New Aster by *Di*/*ign*
Cover design by *Di*/*ign*
Illustrations by Chris Morgan
Printed by Brown Prior Anderson

Notes The Notes section at the back of this book contains useful additional information and references to quoted material in the text. Each reference is linked to the text by its relevant page number and an identifying line entry.

Photo credits The author wishes to acknowledge the following for their kind contribution of photographs: Francis Andrijich (the Beazleys), Bill Bachman (the Wintons), the Office of the Prime Minister (the Howards), Brendan Read and *The Australian Women's Weekly* (the Andersons), West Australian Newspapers Ltd (the Comettis, Courts, Edwards and Newman), Allsports (Geoff Marsh) and *The Age* (Gustav Nossal).

Other Finch titles can be viewed at www.finch.com.au

Contents

Preface

The interviewees in this book are listed below in alphabetical order. I have also included the names of their children – without them there would be no contribution from their dads. Also, they loved the idea that they would see their names in print in a book. Partners' names are listed if they were part of the whole interview, otherwise they are mentioned in the text. Their professions are not listed here but are described in the text where appropriate.

'Anonymous' represents around 22 different individuals from many different backgrounds. Some are named below and are only anonymous for specific quotes. However, a number of interviewees preferred to remain totally anonymous and thus are not named here at all. Their professions are listed except where that might compromise anonymity. To preserve anonymity in some contexts a name has actually been changed in the text rather than being deleted – this was rare.

The interviewees

Aberle, Doug. *Engineer and Network General Manager, Western Power Corporation. Father of Alex and Erin.*

Anderson, John. *Father of Jessica, Nicholas, Georgina and Laura. Farmer. Deputy Prime Minister. Leader of the National Party.*

Anderson, Jessica. *Daughter of John.*

Anderson, Julia. *Wife of John.*

Annus, Susie. *Wife of Kim Beazley.*

Arthur, Ray. *Father of Nerali, Scott and Corinne. Pig farmer, builder, clergyman.*

Arthur, Corinne and Scott. *Daughter and son of Ray.*

Azzani, Salam. *Refugee from Iraq. Son of Sadiq, long-distance truckdriver.*

Bannan, Paul. *Father of Elliot, Nicholas and Thomas. Neurosurgeon.*

Bannan, Alison. *Wife of Paul.*

Barber, Bill. *Plumber. Former sailor in the merchant navy – torpedoed and sunk twice.*

Barrett, Graham. *Ophthalmologist. Father of Trenton and Cameron.*

Barter, Graham. *Nursing assistant.*

Beale, Gillian. *Wife of Chris,mechanic, who died suddenly, July, 2000.*

Beale, Melissa and Trenton. *Children of Chris.*

Beazley, Kim. *Father of Jessica, Hannah and Rachel. Leader of the Federal Opposition.*

Beazley, Jessica and Hannah. *Daughters of Kim.*

Begley, Glenn. *Father of Jonathan, Ryan, Joel and Matthew. Director, WA Institute for Medical Research.*

Begley, Jonathan. *Son of Glenn.*

Begley, Merrin. *Wife of Glenn.*

Biddulph, Steve. *Father and highly acclaimed author.*

Bolton, Mick. *Construction worker.*

Brayshaw, Ian. *Father of Mark, Jamie, Sally and Robert. Sports journalist, Channel 10. Famously took all 10 wickets in a Sheffield Shield innings. Author of* Caught Marsh, Bowled Lillee *and other books.*

Brayshaw, Joan. *Wife of Ian.*

Capelinha, Jim. *Father of Jesse. Marine trimmer/upholsterer.*

Capelinha, JoAnne. *Wife of Jim, daughter of Graeme and Maxine Smith.*

Carnley, Peter. *Father of Ben and Sarah. Archbishop. Anglican Primate of Australia.*

Chaney, Michael. *Father of Kate, Tom, Anna and Amelia. Managing Director, Wesfarmers Pty Ltd.*

Chaney, Anna. *Daughter of Michael.*

Chapple, Allan. *Father of Elizabeth, Rebecca and Tim. Principal, Trinity Theological College. Has lived in England, Malaysia and Australia.*

Chapple, Alison. *Wife of Allan.*

Chappell, Peter. *Father of David, Tim, Debbie and Jeremy. Retired doctor and World War II Spitfire pilot.*

Clare, Alan. *Father of Hamish and Piper. Geologist.*

Clough, Harold. *Father of Susan, Jock, Rebecca, Elizabeth, Billy and Mimi. Director, Clough Engineering. Listed in* Business Review Weekly's *'Rich 200' list.*

Clough, Margaret. *Wife of Harold.*

Clough, Bill and Jock. *Sons of Harold.*

Cometti, Dennis. *Father of Ricki and Mark. Channel Seven sports commentator. Author of* Back to the Time, Back to the Place.

Cometti, Velia. *Wife of Dennis.*

Constable, Ian. *Father of Ben and Jason. Director, Lions Eye Institute.*

Constable, Liz. *Wife of Ian.*

Cooke, Tony. *Father of Molly and Ella. President, Trades and Labor Council of WA.*

Cooke, Jane. *Partner of Tony.*

Costello, Tim. *Father of Claire, Elliot and Martin. Lawyer. Baptist pastor. Former Mayor of St Kilda. Author of* Streets of Hope *and other books.*

Costello, Merridie. *Wife of Tim.*

Cormack, Wayne. *Father of Elly-Jay, Declan and Annie. Music store proprietor.*

Court, Richard. *Father of Kris, Billie and Emma. Member for Nedlands and ex-Premier of WA.*

Creelman, Geoff. *Father of Naomi, David and Ben. Consulting manager in computing.*

Creelman, Alice. *Wife of Geoff.*

Creelman, Naomi, David and Ben. *Children of Geoff.*

De Blanc, Peter. *Father of Belinda, Amanda and Willem. Stepfather of Hannah and Monique. Computer systems manager.*

De Blanc, Yvonne. *Wife of Peter.*

DeGaris, Nick. *Real Estate agent.*

Dickson, John. *Father of Joshua and Sophie. Musician, performer, author and youth pastor.*

Divett, Ross. *Retired Federal public servant.*

Divett, Vanessa. *Wife of Ross.*

Dodson, Alex. *Plumber and sprinkler system installer.*

Doherty, Seamus. *Plumber and union official.*

Edwards, Brian. *Father of Michael, Christopher and Susie. Physiotherapist, pilot and vigneron. Author of* The Matilda Mission *describing his epic solo flight from England to Australia in a Tiger Moth.*

Edwards, Jenny. *Wife of Brian.*

Edwards, Mark. *Father of Rebecca, Paul, Jennifer and Kimberley. Cardiothoracic surgeon.*

Edwards, Kim. *Son of Mark.*

Finch, Rex. *Father of Luc and Zoe. Publisher.*

Fong, Neale. *Father of Ashleigh, Sam, Jack and Lucy. Hospital Chief Executive. Chaplain to the West Coast Eagles AFL football team.*

Fong, Peta. *Wife of Neale.*

Frazer, Ian. *Father of Jennifer, Callum and Andrew. Doctor and medical researcher.*

Gallop, Geoff. *Father of Tom and Leo. Member for Victoria Park and Premier of WA.*

Gangemi, Patrick. *Father of Elsie and Jack. Builder.*

Good, Michael. *Father of Matthew, Sarah, Elizabeth, Daniel, PJ, Mary, Tim and Naomi. Director, Queensland Institute for Medical Research.*

Green, Murray. *Father of Simeon and Andrew. State Manager, ABC Radio, Victoria.*

Green, Poh Noy. *Wife of Murray.*

Harvey, Stephen. *Architect.*

Hayward, Harley. *Father of Quintella. Aboriginal church leader.*

Hill, Danny. *Businessman. Father of Caroline, Ashley, Didi and Felix.*

Huseini, Qatan. *Refugee from Iraq.*

Howard, John. *Father of Melanie, Tim and Richard. Prime Minister of Australia.*

Inverarity, John. *Father of Alison and Kate. Principal, Hale School. Scored over 11,000 Sheffield Shield runs, captained South Australia and Western Australia and played six Test matches.*

Inverarity, Jane. *Wife of John.*

Jeffery, Ian. *Father of Guy, Ruth and Douglas. Architect.*

Kenneally, Mick. *Plumber.*

Kinsella, Mary. *Union official.*

Kolbe, John. *Father of James and Emma. Physician, Auckland.*

Lamb, Clyde. *Father of Dwayne, Jason Wesley and Adam. Former postman and delicatessen proprietor.*

Lamb, Rosemary. *Wife of Clyde.*

Le Souef, Peter. *Father of Tim, Anna and Kate. Professor of Paediatrics.*

Le Souef, Susan. *Lawyer and nurse. Wife of Peter.*

Leeming, Susan. *Human Resources Consultant, EnVision Growth and Change Processes.*

Lewis, Rod. *Father of Anna, Andrew and Clare. Accountant.*

Lill, Michael. *Head, Haematology, Cedar Sinai Hospital, Los Angeles.*

Lillee, Dennis. *Father of Adam and Dean. Former Australian Test cricket fast bowling record holder.*

Lillee, Adam. *Son of Dennis.*

Malcolm, Matt. *Youth worker.*

Malthouse, Michael. *Father of Christi, Danni, Cain and Troy. Coach, Collingwood AFL football club. Former coach of Footscray and the West Coast Eagles and VFL player.*

Marsh, Geoff. *Father of Shaun, Melissa and Mitchell. Former Australian Test cricket vice-captain and coach. Played 50 Test matches.*

Marsh, Michelle. *Wife of Geoff.*

Marsh, Shaun and Melissa. *Son and daughter of Geoff.*

McAullay, Ken. *Father of Sarah, Gabby and Libby. Corporate manager, played State football and State cricket.*

McCluskey, Jim. *Father of Daniel and Georgia. Medical researcher, doctor, Professor and Head of Department, University of Melbourne.*

McCluskey, Eva. *Wife of Jim.*

McCluskey, Daniel and Georgia. *Children of Jim.*

McSkimming, Betty. *Business manager.*

Newman, Peter. *Father of Christie, Rene and Sam. Professor and Director, Institute for Sustainability and Technology Policy, Murdoch University. Co-author of* Sustainability and Cities.

Newman, Jan. *Wife of Peter.*

Nossal, Gus. *Father of Katrina, Michael, Brigid and Stephen. Former Director Walter and Eliza Hall Institute for Medical Research, Melbourne. Chairman of the Reconciliation Council. Australian of the Year 2000.*

Nugent, Chris. *Plumber.*

Packer, Mimi. *Daughter of Harold Clough.*

Pocock, David. *Father of Elizabeth, Sarah, Edward and Harriet. Investment adviser, England.*

Perkins, Harry. *Father of Deborah, Jane and Charles. Chairman of the Board, Wesfarmers Pty Ltd, Chancellor, Curtin University, Chairman WA Institute for Medical Research.*

Perkins, Jane. *Daughter of Harry.*

Perkins, Margaret. *Wife of Harry.*

Petre, Daniel. *Executive Chairman, ecorp. Author of* Father Time *and* Father and Child.

Price, Chris. *Wife of Geoff.*

Price, Geoff. *Counsellor, psychotherapist. Former businessman. Father of Patrick and Ben.*

Price, Patrick. *Son of Geoff.*

Prout, Peter. *Father of Katie, Sarah and Rachel. Lecturer in Education, schoolteacher, pastor, former school principal.*

Prout, Phyllis. *Wife of Peter.*

Prout, Sarah. *Daughter of Peter.*

Raffel, Kanishka. *Father of Hannah and Lucy. Former lawyer. Anglican Church Rector.*

Raffel, Cailey. *Wife of Kanishka.*

Reynolds, Warren. *Businessman and aerobatics pilot.*

Robinson, Ian. *Father of Tom, Sam and Charis. Minister, Uniting Church, Chatswood and Willoughby.*

Robinson, Jacqueline. *Daughter of Charles, Spitfire pilot, missionary and pastor.*

Robinson, Margaret. *Daughter of Jack, Pastor.*

Robinson, Simon, Scott and Amy. *Children of Bruce.*

Schwass, Tim. *Father of Fred and Nick. Lawyer, magistrate, ocean fisherman.*

Seccombe, David. *Father of Daniel, Ruth, Charis and Debra. Principal, George Whitfield College, Capetown.*

Serjeant, Craig. *Father of Tim, Shari and Gemma. Former Australian Test cricket vice-captain. Businessman and pharmacist.*

Serjeant, Julie. *Wife of Craig.*

Serjeant, Tim. *Son of Craig.*

Smith, Brian. *Father of Nicole. Accountant.*

Smith, Robyn. *Wife of Brian.*

Smith, Graeme. *Father of Nathan, Jo-Anne and Michael. Stonemason.*

Smith, Maxine. *Wife of Graeme.*

Sweetman, Eric. *Former WWII prisoner of war, Burma Railway.*

Tang, Eric. *Father of Marion, Melvin, Genevieve and Michael. Nurse.*

Tang, Kuan. *Wife of Eric.*

Thomson, Michael. *Father of Sam, James and David. Sports journalist, Channel 9. Co-host of 'Just Add Water'.*

Timmis, Ben. *Radiologist, London. Father of Guy.*

Timms, John. *Father of Rose, Phil, Heather and Jonathan. Builder. Retired overseas teacher/church worker.*

Vidler, Rebecca. *Daughter of Harold.*

Vojakovic, Robert. *Former refugee and miner. President, Asbestos Diseases Society of Australia.*

Wade, Greg. *Father of Kyle, Paige and Porcia. Cleaning contracter.*

Wade, Chris. *Wife of Greg.*

Watt, Ken. *Father of Emma, Sam and Mandy. Dentist.*

Weller, Tony. *Schoolteacher. Died 2001.*

Willoughby, Tim. *Stepfather of Jessica and Isabelle. Father of Angus and Nina. Stockbroker and triple*

Olympian. *Former Kings Cup rowing coach.*

Willoughby, Anne-Louise. *Wife of Tim.*

Winton, Tim. *Father of Jesse, Harry and Alice. Author of* Cloudstreet, The Riders *and many other works. Shortlisted for the Booker Prize and winner of the Miles Franklin Award and Commonwealth Writers Prize. Larrikin and beachlover.*

Wood, David. *Orthopaedic surgeon.*

Why the interviews of other men in this book?

When I started this book I wrote some text and included my own experiences and ideas but it sounded a bit one-dimensional. After all, I was only one man, with one particular personality and experience of life. I had only one father and have only three children, each with their own unique personality. These were not sufficiently representative of a broader range of fathers.

To avoid this problem I decided to look at statistics on fathering – as a medical scientist, statistics are second nature to me. But useful as they are, they are quite dry, and lack the personal element that we all need to be able to relate to the issues. Also, I noticed a lot of inaccuracy or even bias in much of the statistical work, meaning that some of the data was of uncertain value.

I tried including a few things that I remembered hearing from other dads that I knew, from friends, from patients or public figures, but that was also limited because it relied on my memory of what they said and was also only my interpretation of those experiences. Realising that I needed a far broader range of more personal experience if the book was going to be really useful, I decided to interview a wide range of busy, successful men from different walks of life.

Overall, from all of these interviews there were many things that were common but there were always lots of individual stories from each dad and gems of ideas that I couldn't wait to get down on paper. I found them helpful, and I hope you do, too.

When I started to write this book I took the view that most busy fathers fail in their job as fathers, so this would be a 'collection of confessions'. Instead, every person I spoke to had lots of good ideas. They spoke frankly about their fathering and the mistakes they had made. They described to me a lot of joy and a lot of heartaches. None felt as though they deserved a gold medal for their fathering. I have no doubt that the ideas and experiences I have included in this book will be helpful to other dads who are still on the journey of fathering at the present time or who plan to start in the future. Some of the most valuable bits of advice are those that start with the phrase, 'If I had my time as a dad all over again, I would ... '

Based on the ideas, experiences and mistakes shared in the interviews, I present to you a number of ideas and strategies for young dads. The goal is to increase the chances that our children will live happy and healthy lives and, when they sit around in middle age listening to others talk about how bad or good their fathers were, our children will say 'my dad was a great dad'.

Some issues the interviewees talked about

- How do I know what it is my kids really need?
- How can I work around my busy schedule to get time with my kids?
- Is 'quantity' or 'quality' of time most important?
- What does 'quality time' mean anyway?
- How can I make the most of the limited time I have?
- How can I make my job and my travel schedule work for me instead of against me in my parenting?
- Is it possible to improve my fathering or do I just do what comes naturally?
- How can I know if I am doing a good job as a dad before it is too late to change?
- How can I help the young fathers that I work with to avoid the mistakes I have made?

How relevant are these interviews to you?

The stories of some fathers will be irrelevant to you – with each topic you may find that you have crossed that particular bridge already, or you may never encounter the issue being discussed. There are some high-profile interviewees and others you will never have heard of. There are all sorts of professions. Please don't make the mistake of judging in advance those which might be relevant to you – I suspect that the relevance to you of what they say will have little to do with their profession and more to do with their personality and life circumstances. The value of having spoken to so many people and included their stories is that there will be something you will relate to, either because you are in the same situation as a parent, your children are in similar situations, or you know someone who might benefit from the advice.

You could treat this book like a supermarket and select what you might like to give a go in your life. If you find only a small proportion of the ideas helpful, then, from my perspective, it will still have been worth all the effort. Because all these ideas have been tried and tested, you know that the chance of them actually working is greater than if they just came out of my head.

Who was interviewed?

To research this book I interviewed about 75 busy fathers from many different walks of life: a pig farmer, a prime minister, plumbers, stonemasons, cleaners, a premier, a postman, carpenters, musicians, Test cricketers, construction workers, an upholsterer, multimillionaires, miners, a biker, schoolteachers, clergy, doctors, mechanics, company directors, builders, directors of medical research institutes, some refugees, a trade union leader, an Olympian, an Australian of the Year, a TV sports commentator, an archbishop, a radio network manager, preachers, a stockbroker and numerous others. Two of those interviewed are listed in the *Business Review Weekly* Rich List, and two others arrived in Australia on rusty boats as refugees.

None of those interviewed felt they had been a perfect dad – most wished they had been able to spend more time with their children, and identified a number of things they would do differently if they had their time over again – but each had impressive insight into their fathering. I also interviewed about 33 of these men's partners and 30 of their children. As each person interviewed was also asked about their experience with their own father, the total number of 'children' interviewed about how their dads went about fathering them was over 130.

Whether I was speaking to the Prime Minister in his office in Sydney, a stonemason around a campfire at the beach or a Test cricketer over a beer in his living room, it was obvious that the same issues faced them all, regardless of their profession. Most interviewees are from Australia, with some from New Zealand, South Africa, the United Kingdom, the United States, Canada, Central Asia and Europe. Again, the same basic issues arise for all of them, regardless of nationality. In some cases an interview with an individual is not based on their experience of being a father but of being the child. They are also listed, but their link to their father – rather than to their children – is listed.

Are the children of all the fathers in this book high achievers?

Some of the fathers interviewed for this book have kids who are very intelligent; others have kids who struggle with learning difficulties at school. There were kids who have had academic and professional success and kids who have failed at a lot of what they have done. Some have kids who are disabled and others have kids who are Olympic athletes. Some of their children think they were great dads and others think their fathers failed them.

They have children who are Caucasian, Aboriginal, Oriental, African or mixed race. They had kids who died from illness or suicide. There are issues of street kids, stealing and some are or have been drug addicts. They have kids who are leaders, dedicated to success, and kids who seem to have no goals in life, kids who are serious and kids who are 'party dudes'. They have kids with heart disease, diabetes, severe asthma, Attention Deficit Disorder (ADD), autism, head injuries and cancer. They have children who are heterosexual and children who are homosexual. Having different or difficult children does not preclude professional success and having 'model children' is clearly not the measurement of successful fathering.

Did these busy, successful dads have great dads themselves?

Some of the men interviewed had fathers who were loving but others had distant, unloving fathers. A number had no father because he died when they were young or abandoned the family. There were fathers who were community leaders, successful and famous and others who were alcoholics, abusive or in gaol. Two of the kindest dads interviewed had fathers who were convicted of murder, one of them a notorious serial killer. If you didn't have a good father yourself, that won't stop you being one.

Effect of the interviews

I found that my own fathering improved because of the interviews. Before I started doing them I thought much more highly of my own fathering than afterwards. I realised that there were a lot of things I could have done with my kids that I did not do. That doesn't mean I did a bad job as a dad, and when you read this book and see what other dads have done, I hope you don't suddenly assume that you have been doing a bad job too. It's just that I want to do a good job, and in talking to these other men I realised I could have done better. That is what this book is about – how we can do better and how we can encourage other men to do the same.

The men interviewed all seemed to enjoy the opportunity of talking about their children. They thought about the issues for days or even weeks afterwards. Some rang me a few days later and told me how much of a positive impact it had had on them.

Introduction

Sometimes my friends are a bit envious, because their dads are too busy with work to spend time with them. They say to me, 'What is it like having such a good dad?'

Melissa Marsh

An unforgettable and sad thing happened to me at a restaurant one evening. It illustrates how important it is to know if we, as fathers, are on the right track or not with our children.

I was dining with a group of people and was talking to a woman across the table from me who, it turned out, was the daughter of a doctor. On further discussion, it turned out that her father was a doctor I knew from my medical student years. I was delighted to meet her because her doctor father was my earliest role model – he was kind and respectful to all the patients and staff, was loved by everybody and always had extra time to talk to anyone who was in need. Whenever he walked into the wards the nursing staff, no matter how flustered and bad-tempered they may have been beforehand, all seemed to calm down and become relaxed. We all considered him a bit of a saint, really. I assumed that he was a wonderful dad.

As I enthusiastically related this to his daughter, a surprising thing happened. Just as I finished enthusing about how he always had time for others, her beautiful face contorted in anger and she stated, 'Yes, but he never had time for us, his own children.'

She then went on to describe how her father put all his energies into his work and neglected his own kids. His failure to be a good father to her was, and remains, a very difficult ongoing issue for her and caused her to resent her father's work.

I wonder what happened to her father? I am sure he did not set out with the intention of overworking and neglecting the emotional needs of his children, leaving them with lifelong emotional difficulties because of it. He made the three common mistakes that we fathers often make.

He gave his work too much of his time

You can give a lot of time to work and still be a good dad, but he did not know when to stop. This book discusses how much time children need and how to make that time available, no matter what work you do.

He gave his work too much of his energy

When he came home he didn't have enough energy left to focus on what his children really needed from him. He may have relied on his wife to meet those needs in the children – that is never enough. This book discusses what it is that children really need from their dads so that we can use our time with them usefully and effectively.

He allowed a contest between work and family

In the end, his work was seen by his children as the enemy of his fathering. It is possible to make your work a friend to your fathering rather than its enemy, and this book discusses some strategies that can be used to make this happen.

Good fathering does make a difference to kids

Fathers have a profound effect on their children whether they like it or not.

The more effort a father puts in, the more effect he is likely to have. It is like an invisible 'computer data link' that goes across from the father to the child. Danny Hill

Being a good father does make a difference – children of absent fathers or emotionally distant fathers are more likely to perform poorly at school, get into trouble with the law, fail in marriage and develop drug addictions. Poor fathering is also a major contributor to poor mental health. Good fathering improves children' chances of being academically successful, creative, productive and healthy.

This link between good fathering and children's outcomes is so strong that it is estimated that if all Australian fathers spent an extra five minutes a day with each of their children, the Australian budget would be saved $5 billion per year in areas related to children's outcomes, especially in the areas of law (less juvenile crime), health (less drug taking), education (children would be more interested in learning and less disruptive) and industry (greater productivity).

When I give talks to men, if I mention our failures as dads, everyone knows what it is that I am talking about. There is a lot of guilt, regret and sense of failure experienced by middle-aged men. Many people feel like that. John Dickson

The accused boy never had an appropriate male role model. The failure of fathers and father figures as a cause of crime is insufficiently recognised in the community. Judge Antoinette Kennedy

What this book is about

This book is about work and fathering, and how the two can work together. It says that if we just think about it a bit and do some planning, work can make us better fathers and better fathering can help us in our work. It is not difficult to get this to happen, but it does take a bit of thought and some work.

This book is about fathers who cannot easily change the way they work – if you are the prime minister and parliament sits until 11 p.m. you can't walk out each night at 5 p.m. just because you would rather be at home playing cricket with your kids on the front lawn. If you play Test cricket for Australia you have to tour overseas for several months of each year, because that is the job – you can't ask the other nations to come to your home town each summer to play just so you don't have to be away from your family. This book is about how you can work around those difficulties and actually improve your fathering.

This book is primarily about individuals who are in paid employment. My observation is that the partners of those I interviewed who were not in paid employment were busy themselves, so many of the issues raised do apply to them as well. Also, the women in paid employment I spoke to in the course of the interviews assured me that they have to deal with most of these issues, too. These included a schoolteacher, a nurse, a photographer, a retail store manager, a business manager, a senior public servant, a social worker, a shopkeeper, a pharmacist, a trade union official, a lawyer, a clinical psychologist, a doctor and a member of parliament.

What this book is *not* about

This book is not about why fathering or manhood is important. There are already a number of excellent books covering those topics, and they are listed in the Resources section at the end of this book. Those books are largely about *why* those things are important. This book is more about *how* to go about doing what needs to be done.

I have omitted a lot of the comments that the fathers made relating other issues, such as what to do on weekends with the children, how to create special memories with them and the power of role models. There was not enough space in this book – maybe I will write about those ideas next. Similarly, I have omitted discussion and comments about fathers and their sons, fathers and their daughters, problems dads can have such as alcoholism, depression, divorce, illness, grief, loneliness, and issues related to how to deal with fame or wealth. There is also not a lot of detail about some of the problems children can have, such as learning difficulties, Attention Deficit Disorder, illness, disability, crime, and drug addiction. These are important issues, but a book like this just can't cover all those topics. The final chapter points the reader to quality resources for each of those issues.

How the book developed

I give a series of lectures to medical students on the subject 'Getting a Life in Medicine', and that is where this book arose. In talking to my students, colleagues and patients I realised that most busy, successful fathers are worried that their schedules might prevent them from doing the things that a father should do to ensure that his children don't end up missing out in any way because of his success. While there are statistics that support that concern, I also noticed that many busy dads had found ways of spending time with their children while still working hard. They also often approached fathering in a more organised or creative way, often born of necessity, than fathers who had more time on their hands.

The other trigger that got me writing this book was the inspiration I felt when talking about two dads in the middle of last year who had both done something a bit unusual: they had made a conscious decision to make their children a priority over their work. One was a patient of mine, Tony Weller, who described how he had to fight his own temptation to be ambitious in deciding to focus on his children instead. What made his description poignant was that he only had a few months to live, and the decision he had made was sure looking pretty wise in retrospect. As most of my cancer patients die regretting not spending more time with their kids, Tony's example was encouraging. The other person was my cousin, Chris Beale, who died unexpectedly at the age of 41. He was a very committed father and the words that his two children spoke at his funeral helped move me to write this book. The comments from/about both of these men are recorded elsewhere in the book but, so that you understand something of my motivation to get dads to do special things with their kids, here are the words from Trenton Beale's eulogy for his dad.

To see him smile one more time.
To hear one of his jokes one
more time.
To give him a hug one more time.
To help him fix the car one
more time.
To speak to him one more time.
To hear him laugh one more time.
For this I would gladly travel
through a black hole
And my determination would
bring me through.
(I didn't write in everything
I wanted to do with you one
more time, but if I had it would
have been a hundred-mile-long
piece of paper) …

Trenton Beale (2000)

Many fathers believe that success at work will automatically
prevent them from getting a good report card from their
children. Often these dads say, 'I just leave most of the parenting
to my wife while I earn the bread.' Although the demands of
work, the lack of time for family and the tiredness that work
generates make it hard to focus on children, there are clearly
many busy fathers who have not only been extremely successful
in their work but have also been very successful as dads.

One question kept crossing my mind as I interviewed busy
men for this book: 'Why are some doing such a great job of
fathering while others are struggling now, or have struggled
in the past?' It was obvious that having a busy job was not the
answer. There were some common themes that gradually
made me see something that I hadn't expected. That is, some
busy, successful people actually do well in their parenting
because of the jobs they do, rather than despite those jobs.
They use their work as an opportunity to do things with their
children and, probably more importantly, they use some of
their work skills in their fathering, and this helps them do a
better job of it. What do I mean by that?

■ **Some fathers make a big effort to involve their kids in their work**

They talk to them about it, take them in to work and actually involve them in the work or, when that is not possible, maintain strong connections with their children while they are working (see chapters 3, 7, and 8).

■ **Some fathers use work strategies to help their fathering**

Whereas some dads just put their brain into neutral at home on weekends, others apply some thought to their fathering – doing the same sort of planning that they would with a work project: 'I want to do a good job with my kids, so what is the goal? What do kids really need? What is the best way to achieve that goal? How will the outcomes be evaluated? What obstacles will need to be overcome to get there? What will I get out of it and what will it cost me?'

Our children will ultimately be the best judges of how well we have done in our fathering role – we'll see the results in what sort of people they turn out to be and what they say about us. The trouble is, they won't have a clear view of it until they are older, often not until they have their own children and begin to reflect on how they themselves were parented. That might help us as grandparents, but is often too late for us to change the way we deal with our own children, unless we do a second round of parenting.

It is impossible to be certain what our children will eventually say about how we went about our fathering, but we know that what we do and don't do does make a big difference to the way they end up. There are ways to go about fathering that help children develop strength in their minds, bodies, emotions and spirits, and there are ways that can weaken and even damage children in each of these areas.

A few false notions that are addressed in this book

■ That work is the enemy of good fathering.
■ That we always know what we are talking about when we talk about 'quality time' versus 'quantity time'.

- That if I just do what my dad did it will be okay ('it worked for him so it should work for me').
- That it is not natural for dads to be so involved in parenting – 'it's just a modern fad'.
- That it is impossible to find time for the kids.
- That we all intuitively know how to father best.

Divorced or separated dads

It is important to make it clear from the beginning that the issues discussed in this book apply to dads whether they are living with their children's mother, living with someone else or living alone. Fourteen of the fathers interviewed for the book were currently or had been separated or divorced, and it was clear that the same issues applied to them. While separation added a lot of difficulties to their fathering role, it often also helped wake them up to the possibilities and pleasures of being more actively involved in the children's lives.

The same points also apply if dad is living at a distance from the children. Most of the ideas listed in the section on 'work travel away from the family', for example, can be applied to dads who live away from their kids. In many places I mention 'talking over issues with your partner or the children's mother'. This suggestion is meant to apply whether the latter is living with you or not.

Mothers and this book

This book is about roles and personalities, not gender, income or race. Of course where both partners are in busy employment the ideas in this book apply to both, and in a relationship where the male is at home and the woman works in paid employment there is a lot that would apply to the woman not the man. It is written as a book about fathers rather than mothers simply because that was my starting point, something I had personal experience in. Also, women have been told how to live their lives by men for many centuries and I did not wish to be one more man doing that.

The women who contributed to each interview are not listed by their own professions/roles but as 'wife/partner of …' simply to link them to the relevant father. In no way did listing them this way intend to diminish the value of their own work.

The book emphasises that fatherlessness causes problems in children, but this is not meant to imply that the mothers who care for these children are failures, nor that single mums need to feel a sense of hopelessness.

I believe there is not enough togetherness between husband and wife in raising children today – too much is left to the mother alone. Mothers are not enough, but that is no slur on the mothers at all. They often do a great job but it's just that having a mother without a father only gives the kids half the opportunities to learn about life that they would otherwise have. Having both a mother and a father is the way it was designed to be.

Harley Hayward

Most men emphasised that the mother had a crucial role in any success they might have had as fathers:

The success of fathering depends to a large extent on the attitude of the mother, which in turn depends on how she is being treated by her husband. If she is supported, loved and feels a part of what is happening then she will reflect positively with the children. Julia tells them how much she loves dad and how much he loves them and explains what I am doing when I am not there. She never expresses bitterness about the fact that I'm too busy to be there. John Anderson

There was not enough space in the book to discuss all that was said by men about the important role that their partners or their own mothers played in their children's development and in their own development as fathers. Here are a few more examples though …

When we first had children, I had to be told what to do by Merrin, who I guessed had learnt it from her father who was a very good dad.

Glen Begley

My father was a bit of a role model but he was more distant than my mother was. She was very insightful and had a much greater effect on me than my father.

John Inverarity

In working with the children's mother in the task of parenting it is vital that her role is respected, her views understood and her needs and difficulties appreciated.

The odds are that when you start fathering you are quite definitely programmed, based on your own background. You therefore need to be generous in accommodating your partner's views. You have to mature very quickly and understand what is in your partner's mind. Danny Hill

At this point it is important to emphasise the need for dads who are reading this to discuss any planned changes in their approach to fathering with their children's mother – whether she is living in the same house or not – and to reach agreement on how these changes could best be made. That is because there is a risk that any sudden change in behaviour, such as picking them up from school and taking them out for an ice cream as a surprise, could inadvertently disrupt the children's schedules – homework, sport, music and so on. This could produce an unnecessary conflict. Also, mothers who are used to enjoying a particular relationship with their children associated with specific activities may, like anyone else, need time to adjust to any major change in their lifestyle.

Surrogate fathers

Because 'father figures' are powerful in any child's life, if Dad is not around then there may be others who can help fill the void, e.g., grandfathers, uncles, schoolteachers and sports coaches.

One of the most powerful influences on my fathering was actually my grandfather. He did a lot of parenting of us when we were smaller. For example, every Friday he would pick us up from school in his grey Jaguar on what became known as 'Pop's Day'. He also made us a pedal car and bought us lollies. He would get down and play with us on the ground even though he was 65 or 70 years of age. Basically, he was just prepared to play with us and engage with us. Doug Aberle

How this book is organised

The book is structured in a way that answers a series of questions, such as 'how can I make better use of my time with the kids?', 'how can I know if I am doing a good job as a dad?', 'what do kids need from their dads?'. It features quotes from fathers throughout. These quotes are not meant to be the definitive truth on the subject – quite the contrary. All of those interviewed made it quite clear that they had tried to do a good job of fathering but they were not perfect. They wanted to pass on their mistakes and regrets, as well as their good ideas, to others. As you will see, occasionally some of the fathers disagree with each other on what is important, which is what you would expect from men with such different backgrounds and life experiences. In general, though, their views are surprisingly similar on most of the issues discussed.

Why me?

There are two things that qualify me to write this book. Firstly, I have a very busy job myself, so I'm writing it from 'inside the fast lane'. I have struggled with all the issues that other people describe in this book. In fact I see myself as very underqualified to tell other people what to do. Being a doctor, though, did make it easier doing the interviews because I have spent 26 years talking to people about their personal issues and they expect to be able to trust me, and know that I will respect their confidentiality.

Secondly, this book is pretty much about advice to young fathers from people who have made mistakes along the way. I guess that also qualifies me to write it.

I have really enjoyed writing this book; or rather I have really enjoyed listening to the ideas and experiences of the men, women and children I interviewed for it. I learnt a huge amount from them, and my hope is that in reading our comments in this book you too will learn a lot. Not only that; I hope you get as much encouragement and inspiration from them as I did – it is one thing to offer advice, but another to discuss your mistakes openly with an unknown group of readers. That took courage, and showed me that these men desperately wanted to help the next generation of dads avoid the mistakes they had made. The fact that these men did not all have wonderful fathers themselves was also encouraging – you can be a good dad no matter what sort of role model you started with.

I hope that when your children are 40 and they sit around talking to their friends about you, they will say 'My dad was a great dad! I am proud of him.'

My dad was my biggest role model. Nowadays, when people tell me that I am like my dad, I feel quite proud.   Geoff Marsh

Dad is cool. He is better than a lot of my friends' dads.

David Creelman

I have a very special dad. I'm very proud of him and I know he loves me. I'm very glad to have a family with a wonderful father.   Jessica Anderson

I made a promise to myself when I was about five that every time I spoke to my dad on the phone I would finish the conversation with an 'I love you!'. That way if anything happened to him on one of his trips my last words to him would always be ones of love. I still do that, to this day.
                                                                Hannah Beazley

The most important thing I would say to other fathers who are starting the journey of fathering is that they need to understand the enormous responsibility they have and the powerful effect that their fathering will have in influencing their children, for good or bad.
                                                                John Inverarity

If a fresh young politician came up to me and asked for advice on how to do a good job as a dad I would say, 'Put your own self aside and make the mental leap that these kids are precious and important. They need you more than you need them. You are there to fulfil their needs not your own'.
                                                                John Anderson

During adolescence the boys of course called us 'dinosaurs' and there were conflicts at times, as you would expect. We always made sure that they were aware

that we loved them and that we would always be there for them. No matter what the conflict was at the time, we would always end the discussion by making sure we said something like, 'We just want you to know we love you so much'.

Dennis Lillee

Kids need to know they are loved for who they are, not for anything else – achievements, looks or anything

Tim Willoughby

Chapter 1

What kids need from their dads

Snapshot

- Understanding children's needs
- Considering your children's needs from their perspective

What do kids really need from fathers? Knowing that would help us know whether we are on track with them. These needs of children apply to both parents, but they are mentioned here under the heading 'what do kids need from their fathers?' simply to get fathers to focus on them, make them a priority in their interactions with their children and not expect the children's mother to 'do it all'.

Why can't you just rely on their mother to fulfil all of your children's needs? Because where there are two parents in the house or where parenting is shared, children are always on the lookout for the signals they get from *both* parents. If it is clear that their mother loves them but they think Dad doesn't, will they end up thinking they are lovable or not? What if their mother accepts them and believes in them but their dad doesn't seem to – will they feel accepted and confident or not? Where there are two parents around, parenting is a job for two, and if you don't do what a dad should do to try to meet those fundamental needs of the children when you are available to do so, no-one else can easily make up for it.

Of course what good fathering can achieve to meet the needs of children and enrich their lives also depends upon many other things, including their personalities, their life circumstances and the effect of their social environment on them.

The main needs of children

This chapter discusses what is known about what kids really need. It is an essential discussion, because if we don't have a clear view of these needs we will, even if we make more time with them, not know how best to spend that time. Let's begin then by discussing what kids need. This description is adapted from studies pioneered by Abraham Maslow.

To feel safe and secure

The most important thing children need is security. Protection and security. The best way you can deliver that is to make them know you love them and that they are number one in your life. John Howard

Dads need to be dependable. Kids need to know that Dad will respond to any situation and try to provide for their physical and emotional needs.
Ray Arthur

Children, like adults, need to feel safe and secure. A safe environment allows kids to be kids – to play, to experiment without criticism, to learn and to grow.

Lack of security produces ongoing low levels of stress which can alter the brain's neurotransmitter balance, particularly involving catecholamines (such as adrenaline) and endorphins (the body's own morphine-like molecules). Stress induces many physiological changes, including increased blood pressure and faster heartbeat, muscle tension and irritability. In other words, insecurity causes an ongoing imbalance of the brain chemicals required for relaxed and efficient mental and physical wellbeing. This has been well described in many situations, its most exaggerated examples being the mental damage caused to children in war zones.

Economic security is not something that children care much about.

The sort of security that children need most relates to emotional and physical safety. The relationship between a parent and a child is one of extreme vulnerability.

We grew up on a farm and my father was always putting me down and abusing me. He was very distant and I felt I couldn't trust him. He made me feel that I was never good enough and I was always afraid of him. I now understand things about my dad and I have totally forgiven him. This is important for my girls to know. But back then, whenever I was in his presence I was scared and tense. I ran away from home at 15 to get away from him.
Peter Prout

I always felt safe with my father. Sometimes I'd go to other kids' houses and instinctively realise that the man in their house was someone to be feared. Kids have a kind of radar for this. I've seen it in my own kids.

Tim Winton

The most important components of security that you can provide your children with are the knowledge that you will not leave them, that you will never abuse them emotionally and that you will always be there to support them.

One way I have learnt to empower my children is to father in reaction to the way I was fathered. I remember clearly having my feelings squashed, being belittled and being shamed by my father. I felt it a lot. My heart goes out to kids who get shamed and belittled because I have vivid memories of it myself.

Doug Aberle

A large proportion of those interviewed told me that loving their children's mother, demonstrating that love for her and showing her respect were crucial elements in generating a feeling of security in their children.

Kids need to see love and affection between their parents. Peta has a saying that goes, 'If we are happy, then they'll be happy.' I think that is basically right.

Neale Fong

Kids need to know that their dad loves their mother. This creates a strong sense of security. Of course I tell them how much I love them but I also tell them how much I love their mother.

Kanishka Raffel

This includes actively praising each other for their parenting.

It's really important for husbands to encourage their wives in their job of mothering, to praise them for their skills and hard work and for mothers to build up and encourage dads. John is really good at it. He continually

reminds me of my worth and of how much he values my being at home as a mother to our children.
Julia Anderson

To know they are loved unconditionally

Unconditional love means being loved regardless of what you say or do. I hope that if any of my children were involved in any criminal activities, had a teenage pregnancy, became drug addicts, became prostitutes, or something similar, they would know that my love for them would continue unconditionally.

It's really special to know how much he loves us.
Jessica Anderson

Dad engenders a sense of love, warmth and fun that always have been and still remain the forces that have combined our two families into one, rather than divided them.
Jessica Beazley

This unconditional love needs to be spoken.

Our advice to any young father is to make sure that you tell your children you love them (Dad has always done that with us).
Melissa Marsh

It's important to tell your kids that you love them. I had difficulty doing that until one day. After Jamie's wedding he came out of the church and we embraced and he said to me, 'I love you, old man.' I found the tears poured out of my eyes. My dad never said that to me and I wouldn't have been able to say it to my kids except for that experience – it empowered me. Now I find it much easier to say 'I love you' – and to express other feelings – to my kids.
Ian Brayshaw

The first time my dad said 'I love you' was the morning of my wedding. I was 23 years old. When he said it my heart was pounding and I cried. Dads need to tell their kids they love them when they are younger and more often.
Jo-Anne Capelinha

Love also needs to be shown.

I've always been really affectionate with the kids. In fact I still hug my son when he goes out and he is 17 years old and a big basketballer. Mark has never been inhibited about giving me a kiss when he goes out, even in front of his mates. I really love that and I think it's really important.

Dennis Cometti

Unconditional love should be individualised. Each of your children needs to know that he or she is loved as an individual. Saying 'I love my kids and they know it' is not enough – a child might sneak through to adulthood never being quite sure if you love them. To be certain that there is no doubt in any of the children's minds, work on showing unconditional love to them as individuals.

Love also means staying 'connected' to each of your children.

The worst thing is silence – bottled-up emotions in the kids and the notion that they 'can't talk to Dad'. Dads must keep the lines of communication open with their kids. That is fundamental. Gus Nossal

If the kids don't want to communicate with you then you need to make the first move. Graham Smith

Unconditionally loving your child provides a strong foundation for success in life.

As a kid I knew I was loved. Never had any doubts. I sometimes think that this security was a great benefit to me in later life. It gave me great confidence. I was more excited than ambitious. Ambition often comes from a kind of anger or hurt. You know, the need to show your parents a thing or two. To have some kind of revenge. So many people

*are driven by this. Even in middle age trying to get their parents'
attention in acts of homage or conquest. I felt that there were quite a
few battles I didn't have to fight. That my parents were my friends, they
were allies.*   Tim Winton

To be 'acceptable'

Being loved is something that should flow from the parent,
that is not dependent upon the child – children should be
able to assume that you love them simply because you gave
birth to them, that you have a kind of a biological obligation
to love them.

Children need to know that you to accept them as human
beings even if you do not like the music they listen to, the way
they dress, the friends they keep, the interests they have and
whether or not they believe the same things you do. They
need you to believe in them as people.

*It took me a
while to realise
that what my
girls needed was
support from
their father
rather than lots
of instructions.
I started off with
the 'usual male
bullshit' of trying
to get them to
stop mucking
around and get
on and do what
I wanted them
to do. They soon told me to stop all of that 'male, left-brain stuff'
and I realised over a period of time that they really needed my support
rather than lectures. I have since learnt that it is best to listen and
ask 'what can I do to help?' rather than telling them what to do. As a
consequence, my wife Judy and I now treat our daughters as our best
friends rather than as children, and it works fine.*   Ken McAullay

Dad has neglected to say in his interview with you how supportive he is of our endeavours, whether they are social, educational or relational. He is wary of offering advice, which is a relief, but he has always been a huge supportive element in my life.   Jessica Beazley

Acceptance also means giving children the freedom to make mistakes.

Being a dad is all about accepting responsibility and having the guts to steer your family through the difficult world. Kids need to learn from their dads that it's okay to fail.   John Anderson

We all knew that Dad would always accept us no matter what.

Mimi Packer

Kids need freedom within boundaries. It is like a tunnel. The edges are solid and you give them freedom to bounce around a bit within those walls as they move ahead.   Danny Hill

My advice to dads is to not be judgemental with their children but give them some freedom. The amount of freedom that you give to each of your children depends upon the personality of each child.   Susie Annus

Letting go has been hard for me. When she reached 21 I knew I had to let her go and make her own mistakes and learn from them.

Harley Hayward

Accepting children as they are means that they do not have to live up to any expectations.

The number one priority in fathering is to make sure that kids know they are accepted regardless of their performance. That is one of the

keys. Our world is performance-driven. Kids will experience this at school, in sport, with girls, everything – only if you perform will you be accepted and liked. But no-one can live up to that ideal. So I bend over backwards to make the kids know that my feelings for them are never based on performance. The other day I got upset with Josh about something and he said to me, 'Dad, do you still love me when I am bad?' That's it. That's the question. I have to give him a clear, categorical answer to that question in my fathering. John Dickson

Nor any private dreams for them …

Don't live out of your children. They have their own lives, which you should encourage. Tim Willoughby

My approach to the children has been to encourage them and give them every opportunity but to never push them and not to seek any pride for myself in any of their performances. Ian Brayshaw

Nor our public sense of embarrassment …

I think I was more worried when they were younger about my embarrassment when they did wrong in public. If I had my time all over again I wouldn't worry about it so much. Ray Arthur

Acceptance of children who have intellectual, physical or emotional difficulties can be a challenge for high-achieving parents.

One of my biggest challenges in life occurred when our first child went to school. With two parents who had university degrees I had always assumed that she would be a bright student. She wasn't. It was hard to hear the

teachers tell us how she was struggling. It was even harder listening to other parents plus relatives brag about their kids' achievements, and initially in such discussions I would stay quiet. But then I realised that she was special and she was mine and I would rather have her than anyone else, so I learnt not to be bashful. I learnt to talk matter-of-factly about how she was doing, what she did well and what she didn't and how talented and special she was in her own unique ways. In fact I'm getting tears in my eyes thinking about her now and how much I love her.

Anonymous, economist

To be liked and valued

This is different from being loved and accepted. Acceptance has a neutral aspect to it. To be liked and valued, however, is a level above this. For example, some fathers differentiated between loving and liking their children. They would make a point of doing things like asking their teenagers for their opinions on things, actually listening to what they say and then discussing it.

This can be expressed in a simple way by emphasising different words in the phrase 'I love you'.

I love you   (look at all I have done for you – you should be grateful)

I *love* you   (what *I* feel)

I love *you*   (you are special)

Being loved is thought to enhance positive neurochemical processes in the brain. There are a number of molecules involved. Their imbalance can lead to depression and suicide. It is worth mentioning one chemical, serotonin, which is a chemical transmitter of signals in a small part of the brain. The anatomy of serotonin release follows a pattern consistent with the symptoms of depression – poor memory function, appetite loss, disordered thinking plus sleep and hormonal changes. Antidepressants often act by increasing the amount of available serotonin.

One of the reasons for the terribly high incidence of adolescent suicide in the community is a sense of hopelessness, combined with the adolescents feeling as though no-one values them or is on their side. That is one of the commonest themes in the suicide notes – 'There is just no-one on my side.'

Kids need more than just love and time. They need to know that we hold them in some sort of respect.   Greg Wade

We need to encourage kids to have their own opinions.   Brian Smith

Fathering starts with love and communication with kids, encouraging them to have their own ideas.   Graham Smith

Kim treats the children as adults. He never talks down to them and never mocks them. It's always clear that he values what they have to say. He treats what they say as being important.   Susie Annus

To have meaning and strong values

Many of the fathers interviewed stressed the importance of fathers in establishing in their children's minds a code of living, a set of values that would provide a solid, reliable roadmap for life or at least a clear boundary for behaviour, beyond which they should not go.

Children need to know what our values are. They need to know where this perimeter fence is, and that as they approach it we will always remind them of it.

Kids need a clearly stated set of values, guidance in their education and a good, solid foundation for life in terms of their spiritual values. That way, no matter what happens to them in their life, they will be able to work their way through it. I believe children need a basic amount of time from their fathers to achieve this.   Harry Perkins

To have hope for the future

It is easy for dads to create a sense of failure or hopelessness in children – by almost innocently telling them that if they don't study hard and pass their exams they won't get a job in the future, for instance. Fathers are in a strong position to pass on a sense of optimism (or pessimism) for the future.

In years gone by it was easier to have a sense of hope – we assumed that we would all be able to get a job, get married, buy a house, and so on. Teenagers in particular do not have that same sense of security for the future now. That sense of hopelessness about the future has been well documented, and is a contributing factor in teenage depression and suicide.

This partly stems from the reality of life: life is much more competitive and there is a high unemployment rate, so you cannot be guaranteed a job. In any case most jobs in today's employment market are not secure. Teachers and parents try to motivate children in their schoolwork by telling them 'if you don't study you will not be able to get a job'. Optimism is partly a learnt thing, and children can be easily imprinted with a sense of either pessimism or optimism about the future.

Dad was always an optimist and an enthusiast. Whatever we said, he would say 'that's brilliant'. He always encouraged us, no matter what the problem was. Dad always embraced change and looked forward to tomorrow and the changes it would bring — I guess that is one of the reasons he has always been successful. Mimi Packer

To be confident in themselves

Children who have had all the confidence knocked out of them by criticism and judgement, even if it was said with the intention of trying to get them to improve, struggle in adult life to ever feel that they are doing a good job at anything, and are more likely to perceive criticism in simple questions and clarifications.

It is important not to shake their confidence. My advice to young dads — give your kids a lot of confidence. Brian Edwards

Daughters need confidence, I think. No, it is more approval, that is what gives them confidence. My dad would do anything for me but he wasn't able to encourage me enough, to tell me that I could achieve anything I wanted. I guess a lot of men from that generation were not really good at giving praise. Praise gives you confidence to go on and achieve even more than you already have. Susie Annus

Children need to know that you believe in them, even if no-one else does.

My father never supported me. I remember when I was twelve years of age and I said to one of my uncles that I was thinking of being a doctor, my father said, 'Don't listen to him. He's just talking big about himself.'

Anonymous, obstetrician

To love learning

Life is about learning. Watch a child explore the world, even in their first few weeks. Children go to school daily and learn new things. As adults they will continually encounter difficult problems at work or in their personal life that need to be solved. If they have acquired a lifelong love of learning, a deep curiosity and a love of challenge, they will be well equipped to handle these problems. In contrast, if they have never had anyone encourage this curiosity and love of learning, they may see these difficulties as roadblocks, not hurdles.

Dads can have a major role in encouraging a love of learning in their children.

A lot of my values and intellectual ideas are introduced by Dad. Dad has instilled in me the need for intellectual pursuit itself in science, in logic and rationality. I am sceptical about aromatherapy, for example, because Dad has stimulated my rational analysis of it. Daniel McCluskey

Because Dad was a natural teacher, the whole of our time with him was a learning experience. He would talk about things social, religious, political, anything really. He would quiz us all the time about the capital cities of other countries. He would discuss the news with us in a way that made it alive. Tim Costello

It is this combination of security, love, acceptance and being valued which provide the foundation for fulfilment in life, or 'self-actualisation', with meaning providing the signposts for life, and confidence and hope providing the energy necessary for life.

You can't rely on someone else to meet those needs

When some dads are confronted with all this information they react by expecting someone else to meet those needs – their children's mother, or their teachers.

Teachers can teach the children a lot, and good teachers can stimulate their curiosity, but they have the children for a short time and in large groups. Also, teaching usually doesn't happen in fun environments such as beaches, mountains and parks – it happens in boring classrooms. No-one has the same opportunity that you do to stimulate in your children a curiosity and love of learning in interesting environments that ensure that the lessons will stay with them forever.

Can't the mother do all of this?

You can't sit back and rely upon the other parent to provide all of those needs. Why not? Because parenting is a job for two, and if you don't do what a dad should do to meet those fundamental needs of the children when you are around and available to do so, no-one else can be guaranteed to make up for it. One parent is likely to be more effective when the other parent cannot be there, for example if they have died.

There are dads who can but don't and dads who can't. I have noticed that World War II widows never complain about the absence of fathers in the upbringing of their children. Those fathers couldn't be there. Kids who know that their fathers can be there but don't come are much more likely to suffer than kids who know their fathers can't be there because they have died. John Anderson

Postscript on needs

There is another useful way for you to understand these needs: just think of *yourself* – you need these things, too.

- *You* also need to feel safe and secure from hurt, betrayal, criticism, dismissal, illness. Do you?
- Who loves *you* regardless of what you do or who you are?
- Who shows *you* love physically?
- When did someone last say to *you* 'I love you'?
- Who tries hard to stay connected to *you* as a friend – who calls you when they haven't heard from you for a while?
- Who sees *you* looking a bit glum and says, 'I'm coming over tonight for a beer to talk with you and see how are you are'?
- Who accepts *you* without expectation or judgement?

- Who really likes and values *you* as a person regardless of what you do for them?
- What are *your* strong values?
- Where did they come from?
- What is the meaning and purpose *you* have in what you do?
- How confident are *you* in yourself?
- What are *your own* hopes for your future?
- Do *you* see problems as learning opportunities or roadblocks?
- Do *you* have a curiosity about everything or only about things related to your work?

Do you find some of these questions a bit scary? It is the same for your children.

Finally, did you get these things from *your* dad? I bet you got some but not others. Did you receive them from your mother? Think of the ones that you wish you had received from your dad. That might help you focus on what it is your own children need from you. How are you doing at showing your children that you love them unconditionally, that you accept them and value their ideas and advice?

Summary

- Children need to be accepted and supported as individuals regardless of their academic success, physical ability, sporting prowess, personality, moods, morals or beliefs. This acceptance is often difficult for high-achieving fathers.

- They need unconditional love.

- They need to be liked and valued as special and valuable people. This is different from being loved – love is not enough. Children need to know that they are liked, that you are interested in their thoughts, ideas and opinions, their appearance and their beliefs.

- Children don't need much economic security, but they do need to feel physically and emotionally safe. They need to know 100 percent for sure that neither of their parents will put them down or hurt them.

- They need a clear sense of our values, rules, hopes and beliefs about life so that they have a roadmap for their early life and boundaries for their behaviour until they are old enough to choose their own.

- These things need to be both spoken and modelled. Words without actions and actions without words create uncertainty and confusion.

- You can't pass the buck to their teachers or their mother – if you are available but you don't do what a dad should do, there will be a gap in their lives.

IDEA FOR ACTION:

Each week schedule one thing to try to meet one of these needs.

I almost view with contempt this notion of quality time. I think it's just a baby-boomer cop-out. To have quality time you've got to have quantity time, because you never know when your kids want to talk to you. You can't appoint a time for quality chats. I've found in my relationship with my children that sometimes just out of the blue they'll want to talk, whereas at other times they prefer to wait.

John Howard

One big change I made to my life when I realised what it took to be a good father was to work less, and also to work from home more often. Now I only work a four-day week and I run my computing service from home. This is important because my wife works, and really we have to share the parenting time.

Peter de Blanc

Chapter 2

Create time
with kids

How much time should dads spend with their kids?

My advice to young dads is this. Whatever you do, don't short-change your family on time. You've got to be there for them.   Brian Edwards

There is no escaping the fact that children need time with their dads. Children do spell love 'T-I-M-E'. But just being there with the kids for long periods ('quantity time') is not enough. And focused time with the kids ('quality time') sounds good too, but it doesn't work by itself. Quantity time is the foundation on which quality time can occur.

We are all working longer hours. Evidence from Morgan & Banks shows that 75 percent of men are working five to ten hours more each week than we did just two years ago. While writing this book another newspaper article caught my eye: 'Families hit by overwork'. It said:

Research shows that more than 50 percent of fathers said long work hours and job inflexibility were preventing them from being the kind of parent they would like to be. Australian dads were spending an average of 47 hours per week at work but Australian men wanted to spend more time with their families. Twenty years ago, men saw their main role as breadwinners, not as childcare givers, but things have changed now. Knowing that men want to make a difference these days is a good start.

The West Australian

Despite these good intentions, a number of studies have actually shown us the awful truth of our lack of focus on our children: on average, each child receives less than fifteen minutes of attention per day. In fact some studies state that it is actually less than two minutes per day if a strict definition is used (giving individual children focused attention, rather than interacting with all the children together). Some dads hardly ever eat a meal with their kids in the evening and are too busy on weekends playing golf, going to sporting events or doing other things to engage with their children.

Many children have no special times to remember with their dads – no shared adventures, no special birthdays, no trips to the bush. Instead, all they remember is Mum taking the kids on holidays because Dad was busy or away again.

Time is one of the most rare and precious commodities for busy people. Children know that too – time spent with children by dads who are busy is much appreciated by kids (even if they don't say so at the time). The time you have 'available for work' will probably be greater if you have a partner who wishes and is able to stay at home, than if both of you work in paid employment and share the parenting load without after-school support.

In addition, the exact place where your time–work balance sits will vary according to your children's ages. They need more of your focused time when they are young, the very time when it is most tempting to work harder as you try to get yourself established.

This book will give you some ideas for how to work around a busy schedule to maximise your fathering, and examples of ways in which this might even be an advantage for your work, but it is not an attempt to justify overwork. If you are way over the top, you need to pull back.

I don't get enough time with my kids because I have a very busy job. I work eleven to twelve hours per day. Work even invades my home time. I aim to put the kids to bed at least three nights out of five but that's a good week. During union campaigns such as the 'Third Wave' I often won't eat or sleep for two to three days. This also occurs with major picket lines and periods like the Patrick Stevedoring waterfront dispute. This creates a terrible conflict in my life between my responsibilities at work and my responsibilities at home. When I am doing it I am partly motivated by the knowledge that I am creating a better future for my children. Tony Cooke

Are your kids really a priority?

Before even thinking about whether you give your children enough time you will need to be clear and honest about where they come on your priority list. This might sound obvious, but we don't always do this. It is your right to decide that your children are not your main priority and that you would just rather be at work – no-one can force you to make any other choice. At least you are being honest. If you do make that choice, you will never have enough quality time with your kids. However, if your children are your priority, there is no getting around the fact that you will need to make some decisions about time.

You can only get control of your time by deciding on your priorities. I only ever had two priorities – they were work and family. I don't think I short-changed the children on time, particularly when they were little and they needed it more. Gus Nossal

Fathering is my highest priority and is ahead of my job. John Anderson

My advice to young fathers who are working too much is to just look at their kids and realise that they are only going to be with you for a tiny amount of time. Peter Newman

I don't suppose anybody ever gets to the deathbed scene wishing they'd spent more time at the office. You only have your kids for a while; they're only small once, so why not enjoy them? Parenting has its drudgery and its stresses and low moments. Kids break your heart and wear you out, but anything that's important will cost you something Tim Winton

My advice for young fathers is to always put family first, ahead of work. If you keep that rule in your mind it makes it easier to make lots of decisions. If you just keep that as a priority it will work well for you. It means that whenever there is a clash, family comes first. I always tell people at work where I am, so there is no mystery about it.
Peter Le Soeuf

Pete never missed anything important with the kids. He was at all their school sports, their assemblies and so on. I hear from lots of mums that their husbands are never there at the kids' functions because they are 'too busy'. Not Pete. He's a really busy doctor but he still comes.
Sue Le Soeuf

People always ask me to list my greatest accomplishments, expecting me to rattle off a bunch of movies I've made, but what I'm proudest of is my kids.
Mel Gibson

What happens if you do not make time for your kids?

If your children are not high on your priority list you won't make time for them. So what? The argument against doing this is that there are clearly defined risks to your kids if you are an absent father. Like all risks, though, they are not inevitabilities – you can always find people who grew up with an absent father and still turned out well.

One quarter of all children in Australia and most other Western countries are raised without their fathers. The absence of fathers increases significantly the likelihood that those children will develop problems. For example, 63 percent of youth suicides are from fatherless homes;

children growing up without fathers are 75 percent more likely to need professional assistance for emotional problems, twice as likely to fall behind at school and 8 times more likely to be in juvenile prisons; 70 percent of teenage pregnancies and adolescents suffering chemical abuse are from families in which the father is not present. But that is the 'public' end of the spectrum.

More common, but more private, is the effect of distant, uninvolved fathers on a child's emotional development. Children whose fathers are distant or absent end up with weaker sexual identities and have less respect for the opposite sex. A huge proportion of adults who suffer from low self-esteem, anxiety, depression, fear, difficulties with relationships, loneliness and/or who lead driven, pointless lives can trace their problems, at least partly, to a distant, emotionally detached father who did not do a good job in his role as dad.

Every day in my job as a psychiatrist I talk to people who have psychological problems, and most of them describe poor relationships with their father as a key factor. We need to get fathering right to give our kids a good chance of being happy and contented. Anonymous, psychiatrist

Fatherlessness is the leading cause of many of society's most pressing problems. The emptiness and void left forever by an absent father is one of the most destructive elements in society. Jenny Shipley

My son has a friend whose father was just never there for him, so this kid has grown up with poor values and qualities. He just doesn't know what to do in life. His father was never there to tell him he was doing a good job or give advice. He is a kid who needed his dad but he wasn't there for him. Now he flits around and never has any direction in life.
Anonymous, businessman

Isn't 'quality time' enough?

It's important to discuss this notion of 'quality time' versus 'quantity of time'. You need both, but when these things are discussed there is often no clear statement of what is meant by the terms, so the discussion is meaningless.

'Quantity of time' means hours spent at home with the children, but it is not enough by itself to meet their needs. Many fathers are around the home a lot of the time but have no input to the children's upbringing nor any significant engagement with the children at a mental, physical, emotional or spiritual level. Indeed, many of the people interviewed who thought their dads had done a bad job actually had fathers around the house for a lot of the time. I guess if you are doing a bad job of fathering and you are around the house a lot, it can only make things worse! Time itself has no particular magic properties if it is not used – no worker can get away with just being at the workplace if they don't do any work and no footballer can justify being out on the ground if they don't get stuck into playing the game. Parenting is the same.

What is 'quality time'? Quality time is not simply a 'photo opportunity', an occasion, a special holiday or time when you can enjoy something exciting with the children. This is the 'Disneyland Instead of Dinner Time' approach. It is also not simply attending their sports and music events and going down to the school to speak to teachers. Those things are important, but they are not enough. True quality time involves attending to the needs of the child. Look back at the list of needs in the previous chapter and ask yourself how much time you spend thinking about what you can do as a dad to help your children with those needs. There are hundreds of ways to meet those needs, but simply being in the same house as your children won't do it. Plenty of dads are around their kids for hours every day and achieve the opposite result. You only really know what quality time means for each of your children when you understand each of your kids and their individual needs.

When one attends anniversaries, funerals, birthdays, and so on, children sometimes describe those special times they had with their dads as memorable events in their lives, almost as 'punctuation marks in life'. Of course, such special events are important in a child's upbringing, but they do not replace ongoing true quality times.

This phrase 'quality time' was very popular a few years ago, but there has been a clear acknowledgement lately that quantity of time is also important. You have to spend a certain quantity of time with the kids to be around for the quality moments to occur. You can't engineer special moments with the children on cue. You can't schedule a meaningful discussion with your kids and expect it to work.

You have to give a child time. Quantity is much more important than busy men ever realised. Quality time is really a myth. Merrin Begley

Quality time alone does not work. The kids soon discovered when I had the 'quality time' look in my eye, when I only had an hour to spend and I was going to come in and ask them about their schoolwork and want to play basketball. Naturally they would disappear. It's only quantity time that allows for quality moments. Tim Costello

I'm unconvinced by the notion of 'quality time'. Time with my father wasn't memorable because he made sure we did exciting and spectacular things together. Mostly we did mundane things. But we did a lot of them. I treasure my childhood because I had quantity time. Time that is not merely occasions. We did a fair bit of camping. There were special moments, of course, but mostly it was just hanging out. Non-verbal stuff. Tim Winton

The talk of 'quality time' is the biggest furphy I've ever heard. Kids need both quality and quantity and there is no way around it. Quality time is important, but it's not enough. Richard Court

For good fathering, time matters. The quality time idea is somewhat overplayed because it doesn't really work in your own time. Those occasions of intimacy and true intellectual experience cannot be contrived – you have to wait for those opportunities. Gus Nossal

You can't impose your own timing on kids. You just have to wait for that moment when they want to talk. It might happen when you're washing up, when you're driving the car or maybe late at night when they walk into your study. Sue Le Soeuf

Both my parents gave us to understand that we were the most important thing in their lives. It takes some doing, some living, to achieve this.

I suspect that, as contemporary parents, we all tend to expect too much – to have every cake and eat it, too. We're at the mercy of our social and material ambitions. Often our kids come off second best to this compulsion to be bigger, richer, groovier. That's why I cringe when I hear that yuppy phrase 'quality time'. So often it's guilt time, obligation time, getting in with the missus time, paying my dues time, being seen to be a good father time. There are men of my generation who spend even less time with their kids than their fathers did. Tim Winton

Kids only expect a fair share of your time

It is not always work that stops children getting enough time with their dads. Leisure time can do it too. It is when children see their dads choosing to go and play golf, go to the races or go onto the Internet in their spare time without involving them that they feel cheated. That's not surprising, really, because it tells them that they are not important, that they are way down the priority list. It doesn't matter if dad says 'I love you' then ignores them – children are too smart to fall for that.

Kids know your time is precious. When you are busy, children are well aware of the value you place on time. Therefore it is even more important for them to receive an adequate amount of your time. They don't expect all your time, and it would not be helpful for them to have it all, but they are certainly aware of your choices. If you choose to spend your precious non-work time doing other things and not focusing on them, they will notice it. By the same token, if you choose to spend your precious non-work time focusing on them, they will be aware of it.

I know that I don't have a lot of time, so the sacrifice of time that I make is important for them. John Anderson

For busy dads, time is at a premium, so when they make the effort, it is an even better signal to the children that they care. Jonathan Begley

The time they need is all of your 'available time'. I have always been very busy, but the kids knew that I didn't have a lot of time and I spent it all with them.

Ian Constable

I made a few decisions to try to spend more time with the children. I quit playing golf and instead attended the children's sporting activities.

Michael Chaney

I was tempted to go and play golf but I decided not to play golf in favour of the kids.

Craig Serjeant

The kids always had priority over any visiting professor and over any weekend activities that I might otherwise have done, such as play golf. I never felt that this was a sacrifice, it's just what we did.

Ian Constable

Dads need to show their kids that they mean something to them. Even if it is not possible to get to everything, it is pretty obvious to the kids whether your father is trying to get to as many of your sporting or musical events as possible – it shows that he really cares.

Jonathan Begley

A man came home from work late, hassled and stressed, and found his 5-year-old son waiting at the door.

'Hi Daddy, can I ask you, how much money do you make per hour?'

'Son, that's none of your business. It's rude to ask.'

'But Dad, I must know.

'If you must know, I make $20 an hour.'

'Dad, can I borrow $9 please?'

The father was furious and told his son that if the only reason he wanted to know how much money his father made was so that he could put the bite on him to buy something then he could march off to his room and go to bed and not be so selfish.

'I work long and hard every day and I don't really have time for this sort of stuff,' he said.

The little boy went quietly to his room and the father, after being angry for a while, finally calmed down and went up to see his son to find out why he needed the $9.

'Are you asleep, son'? he asked.

'No Daddy, I'm awake,' replied the boy.

'Maybe I was a bit hard on you. I've been a bit stressed lately. Here's the $9 you asked for.'

The little boy sat up beaming. 'Oh thank you, Daddy,' he said. Then he pulled out some more crumpled-up bills. The father, seeing that he already had money, started to get angry again as the boy started to count out his money.

'Why do you want more money if you've already got some?' the father grumbled.

'Because I didn't have enough, but I do now,' the little boy replied. 'Daddy, I have $20 now. Can I buy an hour of your time?'
                                    Anonymous

CONSIDER THIS:

For how many minutes per day do you give each of your children your undivided attention?

0   2   4   8   10   12   14   16   18   20

- Where do your children fit on your priority list in relation to money, power, glory, the 'meaning' your work gives you?
- Where do they fit in with respect to your leisure activities, your money and your friends?
- What would you be prepared to sacrifice for them?
- Do you show your children that you want to be with them, that it is not a chore for you?

Working from home

During the week I think I have a problem because I take time for granted. I work a lot from home and I struggle a lot with how to create a division between home life and work life.   Kanishka Raffel

Some jobs are typically done largely from home – computer consultant, network marketer, writer, sales representative and pastor. With flexible work hours, the Internet, mobile phones, laptops and fax machines, there is a trend for more and more workers to do their work at home. As well as deciding if you would be able to work from home effectively, if it is an option for you (not everyone can), it is also important to have a clear view of some of the ways in which such a change might impact on your fathering.

If you work from home you need to draw a clear line between work life and home life. This can be very hard, and you can end up feeling that you do neither your work nor your fathering very well, which is quite unsatisfying.

▦ Set a finishing time

I try to let the girls interrupt me if I can and I stop working and focus on them. I want to make them feel like work is never more important than they are. Trouble is, I still don't have a proper finishing time, and therefore it's hard to create that division between work and home. It was much easier when I was working as a lawyer in an office. Kanishka Raffel

▦ Define your work time, and only work then

I had a friend who was doing a PhD at home and she succeeded by making deals with her kids. She would say 'for the next two hours I won't interrupt you and you won't interrupt me, but after that we will all go out together for an ice cream'. Jacqui Robinson

Jess didn't sleep much day or night. I used to fit my work schedule around his naps. I wrote two books on daily bursts of 90 minutes. It was an education in terms of discipline (focusing the mind within a compressed timeframe). Tim Winton

I had to ensure I did not work too many hours each day. My tendency was to go back into the office after dinner if I was working to a deadline. It was hard to switch off as all the things preying on my mind were sitting in the next room! Rex Finch

Working from home can be a way to get more time with the family but you have to make sure you structure the day to ensure the work is done also. I work from home two days a week. For that to succeed, though, I have to structure my time. For example, I like to take the children to school in the morning but then I work between say 8.30 and 10.30 a.m. During that time I am not available for just free-flowing interaction with the children.

I arrange conference calls for that time and answer emails, etc. After 10.30 I go with my youngest to Panda Time (a kind of kindy gym) for about one and a half hours and then between about 1.00 and 3.00 I work again, when again I am not available to the kids. After 3 p.m. I pick up the children from school and hang out with them. I then go back to my study to do more work.   Daniel Petre

I asked my son, Patrick, what he thought the traps were of my working from home.
Patrick: *You can get too lazy. You can talk yourself out of doing something and allow yourself to get distracted.*   Geoff Price

Focus on the children when you are with them

Because there is no dividing line between home and work it is easy to become more mentally absent. You can't switch off at home like blokes who come home from work can do. For me there is no gap between leisure and work. Even when I'm working, they come into my study to talk to me, and I allow that.   Ian Robinson

I've always been at home a lot, and I collide with the kids a lot that way. I'm not so sure that's good, though – it means I don't always focus on them as much as a bloke who is out working all day and then comes in and gives the kids his undivided attention.   David Seccombe

Even when I was working at home I was always accessible to them. I wouldn't ever lock myself away in the study. They wouldn't ever feel that when I was at home I wasn't available.   John Howard

Getting a balanced combination of both approaches, working at home and away in a workplace, is one way of gaining the benefits of both worlds, provided your work can be compartmentalised successfully that way and provided you are disciplined enough to stick with it.

When working from home starts to create tension in your children it may be time to rethink how you are doing things.

Our impetus to move the business out of home came one afternoon when my son returned from school to find three phones ringing, his two parents working busily in one room and two freelancers in the lounge and dining rooms. He walked into the office and said, 'Dad, this is getting ridiculous!'
Rex Finch

The way I work is to spend the mornings at home and afternoons at work. At home I limit my work to thinking, researching, writing etc. Then I work in the office in the afternoon and do administration tasks and have meetings. That way I can still come home at the end of the day and have that 'coming home feeling' rather than feeling like I am returning to my office. Because of the way I have structured it I don't come home to emails, phone calls and meetings – those have been handled at the office.

John Dickson

Working from home is difficult, but it can be very rewarding if the problems listed above can be worked through.

Kids learn about working styles and attitudes at close hand.

I was interested in whether my working from home had an effect on my children's ideas about work. So I asked Patrick.
Patrick: Not much, Dad. There's more effect when you're younger and views are forming and there's someone home to guide them. Then they are not overly affected by society's usual view that men work 9 to 5, and it reinforces that there are many ways to make a living.

Geoff Price

My kids were twelve and thirteen when I lost my job and began a business from home. Looking back, I can see how important it has been for them to see me pick myself up and start again. They could witness the daily issues in the business and see first-hand how I confronted impediments big and small – from setting up computers to organising the daily run to the post office. Consequently they saw me in all my moods, learnt to economise and shared the exhilaration of our first success.

Rex Finch

Flexibility in lifestyle is one of the biggest advantages.

My wife, Chris, and my son, Pat, gave me their views on my working from home.
Patrick: It's good, but I don't remember it any other way, it seems you've always been at home. The best thing is you're flexible, not at work all day and night, and you're around a bit, I suppose. The worst thing is that when you have clients I have to be quiet if I'm in my room.
Chris: It's more flexible for me, you're available to do things with the boys, like this week when you took them both to lunch. And you hang the washing out. It makes you more contented and the boys see different ways of working.

I chatted with Pat about what he thought the effects were on my younger son, Ben.
Patrick: *When he's sick you can take him to the doctor and keep an eye on him; and make sure he's not watching TV all day.*   Geoff Price

Working from home has both positive and negative aspects. If you are working from home, you are particularly able to be available, and when they need something for a school project and it is the last minute (which it usually is!) – 'Dad, I desperately need something for tonight'– then we can shoot into Chatswood together and do some shopping.   Ian Robinson

In the years before my wife joined the business, I was the available parent in the mornings and after school. This meant I drove them to school with their projects, took them to the shops if there was something important to buy, and collected them from school if they were sick. We had more time together than ever before and so got to speak about all sorts of issues. I also became a regular cook and did the shopping. I think it was important for the kids to see how my wife and I handled the new roles. I really enjoyed the cooking: the kids could see my cooking style was part inspiration and part experimentation (usually edible).   Rex Finch

A great thing for me is that I have much more flexibility to respond to the weather when a beautiful day or an exciting storm invites me outside. And to listen to my own inner voice when it whispers to me to do the things I love to do to nurture myself and pursue my own inner life. Then there is the satisfaction of knowing that I am choosing my own way of expressing myself through work and that it works for me and my family.
      Geoff Price

Not everyone can work from home well; be prepared for that.

For many years I worked from home. It took longer than it should have, but I finally realised that I can't have my place of work and my home as the same place. I personally can't switch very well. In the end I don't do either my work or my fathering well in that situation.   Allan Chapple

Summary

- Time with kids is essential for good fathering.

- Some dads spend less than two minutes per day focusing on their kids.

- Many men *say* their kids are a priority but their actions show otherwise.

- Being an absent father puts your kids at increased risk of emotional, educational, criminal and health problems.

- Quantity of time cannot stand alone – hours spent at home can be wasted.

- Quality time cannot stand alone – you can't engineer special times with kids; mostly they just happen and you have to be around for them.

- You need both quantity and quality times for good fathering.

- Children need to know that you enjoy being with them.

- Children simply expect their fair share of your available time.

- Working from home increases your time with the children, but not always in a way that allows you to focus on them.

- Draw a clear line between work life and home life.

- Working from home can be very rewarding if the problems can be resolved.

- Not everyone can work from home well; be prepared for that.

IDEA FOR ACTION:

Work out how many hours in the week you need to sleep, eat and work. How many hours are left for your children? Could you use that time better than you do now?

When I am home I try to take Rachel to school and often pick her up as well. I'm told that I'm one of the dads most commonly seen at the school because of course a lot of the other dads never take their kids to the school at any time.

Kim Beazley

When the kids were young we lived on a farm and the kids were not sent to boarding school. That meant they were always around and helped on the farm. They helped with animals, ploughing, lots of things really. In fact our time on the farm really formed the pattern of our family life – they were just always part of our working lives.

Ray Arthur

Chapter 3

Make time for kids – on workdays

Snapshot

- Being flexible with working hours
- How to be accessible to your children when at work

I don't see my three young sons awake between Sunday night when they are put to bed through to Saturday morning when they wake up – I leave for work each day before they wake up and I'm at home each night after they have gone to bed. One of the boys is starting to get into trouble in the neighbourhood and I know what you think the reason is likely to be. It's hard to change it, though. Anonymous, doctor

Given that there are only 24 hours in everyone's day, how have the other dads interviewed stretched their time during the week to make sure they spend quantity and quality time with their children?

Changing the shape of your time

The amount of time that you have to spend with your family during the week is highly variable – there are some jobs that make it very difficult for dads to spend time with their family at either end of the day. Some start early in the morning:

Time during the week is a problem for me. As a stockbroker I start work early. The market opens at 7 a.m. – I really wish I could have those early mornings over breakfast with the family. Tim Willoughby

Others are irregular during the week. For men in such jobs the weekends and special times are more important.

Monday to Friday have been pretty useless for us. On weekends, though, I was always there for all their sporting events. I also went on their school sports trips. Ian Constable

Nevertheless, it is possible for most dads to work around their schedules in order to maximise time during the week with their children. Here are some suggestions.

Starting and finishing times

We tend to have fairly fixed starting and finishing times in our work. Sometimes this is set by the workplace, but more often than not it is because we are creatures of habit. Some people's working week is pretty inflexible, but for many it is not. If you haven't thought about it already, I'd like to introduce you to the concept of 'changing the shape of your time'. It is a development of flexitime, but it is focused on family, not leisure. This point is illustrated in the following figures:

Fixed 'shape of time'

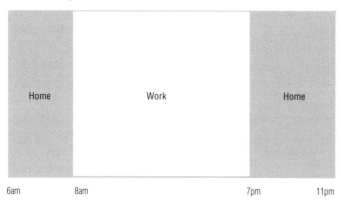

Flexible 'shape of time'

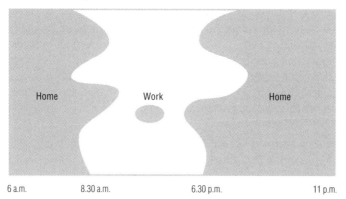

If you loosen up your idea of a working day, then without any nett loss of hours worked, it is possible to generate better times with the children. You can alter the shape of your working week so that, for example, you start earlier one day and finish later the next day, enabling you to spend more time with your family on at least one of those mornings. Why not get up and start work at 5 a.m. one day then wait until 11 a.m. the next day before going in?

Start work later on one or two days per week. Would your life be vastly different if you started an hour or so later once or twice a week? Walk or drive to school with the children and kick a football or throw a netball with them in the playground. Go to their assemblies, visit their classrooms. This doesn't have to happen every day, but why not once or twice a week?

Similarly, it may be possible to finish early some days – and attend your children's sporting events, or even coach the team – and make up for it on following days. If you do have to work late for a meeting, come home early the next day to make up for it. Why not go back to work and do another two hours' work one night then leave two hours earlier on another day during the week?

In some jobs you can even work from home on one or more days of the week.

At this stage of my career I am very fortunate in terms of an ability to create flexibility. Each week I do my office work from Monday to Wednesday and work from home on Thursday and Friday. I also work for The Children's Hospital at Westmead on their Council and fundraising, and I include that as part of my 'working week'. I am lucky I can structure my week to do this, but many men can't do that. Daniel Petre

It is also possible to create 'holes' in your working week where you leave work to call in at home or to attend the school for your child's assemblies, music performances, sporting events, parent–teacher interviews, canteen duty and so on during the day, and then make up for it at other times. Of course that is harder, and sometimes impossible, if you live a long way from work, but many men can do it if they choose to.

My work as a carpenter has always allowed me to spend extra time during the day with Cherith and the kids. I deliberately chose things that way. I often get home for lunch or call in at other times during the day between jobs.

Patrick Gangemi

So even before you begin to address the issue of sacrificing some of your work time for your family, simply changing the shape of your working week will enable you to follow a lot of the suggestions made in the next few sections. Of course for some workers all of this is just not possible because the employment situation does not permit it. Where it is possible, though, which is in the majority of jobs, it is a good idea.

I used to start work early in the morning because it was a great time to get work done without being interrupted by the telephone. Then I had a severe accident and re-evaluated my priorities in life. I decided to start walking to school with the children each morning. That's one of the best decisions I have ever made – I have loved every second of walking to school with them, and I have done it for about the last ten years as each child has come through the school. Mostly we just talk about nothing and sometimes when I get to the school I kick a football with them, visit their classroom and find out where they are sitting, look at some of their work, speak to the teacher, muck around with some of their friends. Sometimes I wouldn't go into the school but would stand and watch them walk into the playground. I would often gaze at them and think of how infinitely precious each of those little bodies was to my soul.

In order to get time to write my books, I get up at 4 o'clock in the morning and stop writing by around 7.00 or 7.30 so that I spend the morning time before school with the kids. It's a temptation to get up and go into my study and work from 7 o'clock but I'd rather pay for it with less sleep for a while and not miss that family time. We all get together in bed and drink tea. We ask the kids to talk about their day, what's going to happen (computing, gym, friends etc) and we have a quick prayer together. That helps them focus.   John Dickson

Making time in the morning

Brain chemical levels alter markedly at different times of the day, a phenomenon known as 'circadian rhythms'. The biology of these circadian rhythms suggests that dopamine, melatonin and cortisol are three of the most important neurotransmitters involved in this. You will have noticed that some people are 'morning people' and some are not, and this is thought to be related to the release in different individuals' brains of different amounts of these molecules. Children (excluding teenagers!) are usually in pretty good shape early in the morning, so this can be a good time to interact with them.

■ **Be involved early in the day**

One of my goals in life is to be around in the morning. Alice is not a morning person so I tend to get up and help the kids with breakfast, help reduce the squabbling amongst the children.   Geoff Creelman

■ **Have breakfast together a few times each week**

I've always been involved with having breakfast with them.
                                                            Dennis Cometti

We have always eaten together, even breakfast.   John Inverarity

I make it a point to always be there at breakfast time.   Peter Le Soeuf

■ **Take them to breakfast as an opportunity for a 'dad date'**

For the last five years I have taken the kids out individually for breakfast. I do it about four times a year. It's not only on the weekends – I'll do it on a school morning, around 7.30 a.m. I never take them to McDonalds because that is just a rush job, but I take them to a proper restaurant.

I let the conversation go with the flow and don't usually have an agenda, although often I will ask things like 'Are you happy at the moment? Do you feel like you are seeing enough of me? Are you enjoying being part of our family? Is there anything you would like to see changed?' – those sorts of questions.
Neale Fong

▩ Drive them to and pick them up from school

I have tried to take the children to school in the morning several times per week.
Mark Edwards

I have found that travelling to school in the car is a great time to be with the kids.
Peter Prout

I take the kids to school early and I pick up some of the kids a few days a week. I find it a good time to ask, 'How are you getting on in the playground with friends? Is anyone causing you problems at school?' This worked out well for Tim with regard to his maths. When we started to talk I asked him, 'How was maths?' He told me it was really easy and somehow I knew there was some trouble, because he wasn't being challenged. Turns out he was in the wrong maths class and I was able to change it at the school.
Craig Serjeant

I leave home at about the same time as the children. I only take them to school about once a week because it's better for them to go by themselves – to walk or ride – because it produces self-reliance. That way if they are late, it is their responsibility, not mine.
Geoff Creelman

A special memory is when I came back from a trip and turned up at my young daughter's school at the end of the day. When she saw me she ran the length of the school playground straight towards me and jumped up and hugged me. That's a special memory.
John Howard

Fathers don't get enough one-on-one time. We have no excuse as dads for not making time once a week or so to pick our kids up from school. That could even be a surprise whereby you take them off for an ice cream afterwards.
Anonymous, businessman

I've made a conscious effort to pick them up after school and many times we'd go for afternoon tea or a snack.
Dennis Cometti

If you decide that your kids are a priority and you have control of your time then it is possible to spend lots of time with them even though you've got a busy job. For example, when Sue was working and couldn't pick the kids up from school, I took three afternoons off per week to pick them up. If I needed time off with them I just did it, no question. Peter Le Soeuf

■ Be involved in early morning sporting (or other) activities

When Ben was at school I used to get up at 5.30 to take him to rowing training. It was a good bonding time together. It gave us a chance to talk together. In fact I felt that I was part of the team, so that when they won the Head of the River it was 'we won the Head of the River'.

Peter Carnley

I tend to use the early part of the day to spend time with the kids. I tend to take the kids to school, early morning water polo practice, and so on. Because the school was a fair distance away, it is a good time for me to get to talk to them. Ian Frazer

I really appreciated the early morning swims we used to do with Dad down in the Swan River at dawn in the summer. Ian Robinson

■ Offer to drive them places

Many dads find that time in the car with their children is the best time for talking to them. While this is listed here under early morning options, of course it applies to any time of the day. It provides an ideal opportunity to have 'shoulder-to-shoulder' time rather than 'face-to-face' time, and children often open up more under such circumstances.

My son and I sometimes load the mountain bikes onto the car then drive up to the mountains behind us and ride on trails for a few hours. To be perfectly honest the best part of the trip is the driving to the mountains and driving home again. I guess it's the anticipation of the adventure that we talk about on the way there and discussing what we both did on the way back. When we are on the trails we are both busy doing our own thing, mostly surviving the ride, so we don't talk as much. John Kolbe

I don't know how you really felt, but I love the chats you and I would have when you would be driving me somewhere. I'll never forget the 'deep and meaningful' conversations we'd have and I'll always treasure them.

Eulogy by Melissa Beale, delivered at her father's funeral

I always try to take my teenage daughter to her sporting activities because it gives me about twenty minutes to talk with her, otherwise we don't get

a chance to talk. That twenty minutes in the car gives me a good chance to laugh with her and talk about inane things. Anonymous, sportsman

It is not only the car that generates such times, but washing up together, fixing something together or doing the cooking together. Can you engineer that into your life a few times per week?

You can't impose on kids your own timing. You just have to wait for that moment when they want to talk. It might happen when you're washing up, when you're driving the car or maybe late at night when they walk into your study. Sue Le Souef

Making time during the working day

To young dads today I would say, 'Don't just react to children's problems, try to plan ahead. Be at all of your children's important events such as the first day at school and school assemblies.' Richard Court

A lot of fathers have no contact with their children from the moment they walk out of the house to go to work until the moment they walk in the door at the end of the day. While in some occupations this is unavoidable, in many there are lots of opportunities to maintain contact with your children during the day. This is really important, because it represents another way that your work can become a friend to your fathering.

Make sure your children have access to you

The more important your job is, the more important your children will feel if they have access to you when no-one else does.

There is a nice scene in the movie *Richie Rich* that illustrates this point. I watched a few moments of the film with the children a few weeks ago, and happened to be there during a segment in it where Richie's father was talking to the President of the USA. Richie rings his father and says, 'Dad, what are you doing?' His father tells him that he is with the President discussing the state of the nation's economy. Richie then starts to tell his dad about his day and his dad listens to him instead of cutting him off, and engages with him. I thought this was a really nice example of fathers trying to make themselves accessible to their children no matter how 'important' their job.

I always give the kids direct access to me when I am at work, even if I have people with me. In fact I have a special phone line on my desk that only the family use. Of course, sometimes when they call it's not convenient for me to talk to them and I let them know that unless it is urgent we need to talk later, but they always know that they have direct access to me. Tim Willoughby

The family always had access to me – they always knew that they were number one top priority, even when I was made a member of the Wesfarmers Board and was very busy. They knew not to bother me if it was trivial, but if it was anything that wasn't trivial and especially if they were emotionally upset, they knew that they had immediate access to me. Harry Perkins

Always be available to your children so that they know they can get hold of you even on the telephone across the other side of the world. Mark Edwards

Because I worked near home the children could always wander down to my office and interact with me. I have always enjoyed children, their humour and the idea of watching them grow and influencing that. I just like doing it, so when I had children, it was just natural for me to want to spend time with them. John Inverarity

Any of my family can call me at any time when I am working. It doesn't matter what's happening. If I'm in a Cabinet meeting and one of my children rings, the staff will get me. Of course if the kids say 'don't disturb him now, it's not that important, just give him a message' they won't disturb me. Mobile phones have really improved communication with children. They are fantastic. John Howard

Tim has always made a big point about accessibility. Whatever is going on for him, nothing precludes the children having access – he may have to call them back or rearrange a schedule, but they know he is approachable at any time. Anne-Louise Willoughby

◾ Call them from work

I really wish I could have those early mornings over breakfast with the family, but stockbroking just starts early. I always ring home in the morning from work and talk with Angus about his day so that he starts it with me 'in his head'. I check in with Anne-Louise and the little one manages to wrestle the phone off them at some point.   Tim Willoughby

With modern mobile phones I can keep in touch with my teenage daughter while she is away at boarding school. Of course she can't use the phone during lessons, but I leave text messages that she gets during breaks, like 'Hope you have a good day', or 'Thinking of you, love Dad'.
                                                                David Pocock

◾ Attend special school events

You probably won't be able to get to every performance, assembly and sports day, but try to get to the ones that are special.

I always try to attend parents' activities and school sports days and make an effort when there is a special reason to attend, such as cross-country running. To do that, I 'write off the morning' in my diary so that my secretary knows not to book anything. I think that is really important, because children need to know that while you cannot be there for everything, you will always try to be there for special events.   Paul Bannan

I think it's important for fathers to support their children. When I won a prize at school, for example, he was there – he had to cancel a lot of stuff but he was there.   Jessica Anderson

The other routine that I've followed fairly rigorously is that if I'd promised my kids that I'd be home for something special I'd always make certain I was.

This is very important. I would often get planes very early in the morning just to get back for school sports or other important events. You really should move heaven and earth to keep any commitment you've made like that to your children. I never promised to be home if I couldn't be and I'd explain that to them. For example, not long after I became Prime Minister I had to go up and look at a drought area in Queensland. My younger son was in a school debate that evening and although I was tired I went to the debate straight from the airport. Richard made a point of saying, 'Thanks. I know you've been in Queensland all day.' John Howard

Although Dad was often away, I always felt that he was available to me and certainly that he would be there for special occasions. One of my vivid memories is winning a running race when I was at primary school. I saw him at the end of a line and after I crossed the line in first place, I just continued running straight past the line and the judges and into his arms. Jock Clough

If you look back and you realise that you missed a lot of their special events, it is not just your children who will have missed out – you will have also short-changed yourself.

My six-year-old daughter is a real delight. Recently she asked if I could ride to school with her and I took her on a practice run to the school, but she had to walk up the last hill. When it came to actually riding to school with her and when we arrived at the last hill there were other children around and she rode straight up the hill as if it were easy. I loved it! And what I really appreciate was the fact that I was there to enjoy it. Richard Court

The best advice I can give to dads is to make sure that you're around the house and that you're involved in your kids' lives and that you're there when it matters. Geoff Gallop

Put these things in your schedule. Don't wait until the last minute and decide whether or not you have time. Make it a fixed item in your diary.

Try to plan a schedule so that you can be at all your children's most important occasions. Richard Court

I put all my kids' stuff on my calendar in the office and it's inviolate. No-one else is going to raise your children and you've only got them for one minute. It was going to be my daughter's last Indian Princess camp-out but there were going to be other elections. Ron Kirk

If you do get involved in a special activity with your children you probably won't have the whole day to spend with them, but try to avoid always making just a cameo appearance. Of course that is the only way it can be done at times, but when you can stay longer, do.

I now have a six-year-old daughter, Emma, and even though I am the Premier I think it's really important for me to make as much time as possible for school events. I try not to rush in and out, but to participate in assemblies, busy bees and if possible I ride to school with her one day a week. Richard Court (in 2000)

▪ Try to involve your children in your work

Another way to make your work less of a foe and more of a friend is to try and involve your children in your work. Quite a number of the fathers interviewed described creative ways in which they involved their children in their paid employment.

One way I succeeded in spending time was to get the boys involved in my research and clinics in Aboriginal communities. Ian Constable

One way to spend time with my kids was to create areas of work that involved them. In my work as a church Minister it was possible to get the kids and their friends together for camping trips, Bible studies and so on. That way I could be with them and be working at the same time. Ray Arthur

If I were to give advice to young dads now based on my father's model, I would tell them to spend quality time with their children, one-on-one, and one of the best ways to do this is to deliberately involve your kids in your working environment, in the same way that Dad did with us.

Jock Clough

During the industrial disputes when I am committed 24 hours per day, we have various ways of involving children. We get T-shirts printed, hire bouncing castles, provide free food and ice cream. We get helium balloons, have family days and overall encourage families to be involved. At our 'embassy site' opposite Government House we had toys, a sandpit, blackboards and chalk, zoos and family barbecues.

Tony Cooke

Dad lets me come into work with him. We either have lunch or go on ward rounds where I get to meet all the patients. Sometimes they give me their choccies. I like seeing the patients, especially Mrs Salvia – she's a special friend.

Amy Robinson

The decision to help set up the new Board of Directors for the Perth WildCats basketball team was done to help a friend. In fact it was a good family time because the kids got to come to training and meet the players and were able to bring friends to the games. I decided up front that I wasn't going to do it if the kids couldn't come. I talked it over with the family before we even made that decision. That way they had ownership of that part of my life.

Tim Willoughby

■ **Tell them about your work pressures.**

If you have to work hard for a particular period of time, explain that to them and involve them in that decision.

I don't think I ever talked to the kids enough about why I was doing what I was doing or what it was all about, for that matter. I just tended not to talk about my work with them, possibly to protect them from being swamped by it. I'm sure I overcompensated.

Allan Chapple

Dad and Mum were always honest about what was happening with Dad's work.

Mimi Packer

We have always tried to let the children know about our struggles and successes at work. Attached are a few examples of that from our Family Breakfast Record Book, a book that recorded quotes from our whole family during Family Breakfasts that we had every Sunday with the kids when they were younger. These examples are included simply to illustrate how we sought to let our kids know about the ups and downs of work.

> One weekend I told the kids about a pending promotion that I was having a bit of a crisis of confidence about ...
>
> *Praise:*   20/11/94
> Peter Prout's 50th birthday last night.
> Simon and Dad planning their 'Rite-of-Passage' hike together.
> Scott and Amy both got merit certificates.
> *Problems:*
> Dad is nervous about his possible promotion to full professor.
> The kids won't sit still.
>
> On another weekend I told them about something special I felt I had done at work ...
>
> *Praise:*   21/3/97
> Simon gybed while windsurfing on Tuesday (he was rapt, shouting and cheering). Dad came over and gave him a hug.
> Dad – feels like he's changed the direction of medical research in Western Australia because he finally, after years of slog, got everyone to agree to having a single medical research institute.
> Scott – got lots of runs in cricket.
> Mum – grateful for nice surprises – getting to know the Dicksons.
> Amy – came first in breaststroke.

■ **Attend some of their school camps**

This can actually be a lot of fun, although it can also be hard work.

■ **Invite them to do your work**

When they are on breaks from school, invite your kids in to have lunch with you and visit you in your place of work.

The kids still come in to work and have lunch with me at least once during their school holidays. I don't normally stop for lunch so it is a bit of a treat for me, too. I get pretty fired up at work, so I have to discipline myself to slow down and be with them and not respond to the urge to get on and do things at those times. I usually let the kids pig out on ice cream, jelly and other non-healthy stuff.

▪ Be flexible enough to stop work and do spontaneous things with the children from time to time

Now that they are teenagers, if they ring during the afternoon because they want to go windsurfing I'll often stop what I'm doing, if possible, and take the opportunity of going with them.　　　Peter Le Soeuf

▪ Be prepared to stop work and be with the children at crisis times, such as visits to the doctor

Don't give the children a signal that it is only mothers who are there for them when they really need someone. Knowing that you have a conflict between work and them, and you choose them can mean a lot to your kids.

Dads need to be around at times that matter – crisis times such as exams, relationship breakdowns and important transition times.　　　Jim McCluskey

My son missed a lot of his Year 6 because we moved about the world a lot that year and he missed out on most of his teaching. It became obvious that he would have to repeat Year 6. I decided as his dad that I would take the responsibility of telling him. To do it I made it into a special event by taking him down to the ice cream shop and discussing it with him. When I broke the news to him he was a bit sad. It was gut-wrenching stuff, because it could have been pretty humiliating for him. But I'm glad I was there to do it as his dad. Thinking back on it, I would hate to think that I hadn't taken that responsibility, but had left it to a teacher.　　　Anonymous, athlete

▪ Do canteen duty at least once a term – it helps destroy the old image of 'men's work' versus 'women's work'

I read in Dan Petre's book that we should think about doing canteen duty. I had never thought about this before but it seemed like a good thing to try. I went along this year expecting to be bored, but it turned out to be great fun. My job was to stand at the entrance to the canteen and shepherd the kids in at regular intervals. I had a great chance to meet lots of them, joke with them about which sporting 'house' was best and whether the girls thought the boys at the school were nice. My daughter told me later that her friends thought I was cool, which was a bit of a relief as I had joked around so much.

■ **Volunteer to take over their mother's role from time to time if she wants a break**

In many relationships, mothers often get no break from their role, even when they are on holidays. Give her a regular break from her tasks.

For a period of time Merrin was getting exhausted in her role as mother. So I took five weeks of annual leave in the form of one day a week, every Wednesday, to look after the children while she went off and did whatever she liked for the day. It might have been shopping, seeing her friends or whatever. We wrote it on our calenders as 'Merrin's Day'.   Glen Begley

Another idea along those lines is for Mum to go away and have 'a holiday from being Mum'. That might mean renting a flat for a few days to do things she doesn't get a chance to do – having a mini-holiday at the beach, going off with friends for a weekend.

My wife decided that she would like to have a break from the routine of mothering from time to time. My job is busy so she does get more than her share of the parenting work load – and she does a wonderful job of it. She goes off to the beach for a few days sometimes and just walks all day. Once she borrowed a friend's flat and took all the photo albums and spent five days getting them up to date. She would come home during the day and call me every day at work, but avoid the morning rush and the night rush. I thought it was a bit strange at first, and so did some of her friends. Now we all think it is a good idea, and the other dads in the community are getting requests for the same thing!

Summary

- We need to loosen up our concept of time and working schedules and be more flexible.

- It is possible, by 'changing the shape of your time' to create extra time for the children without necessarily losing any work time.

- Start work later once or twice a week, and do things with the children instead.

- Use travelling in the car with them as a chance to talk.

- Make sure the children feel they have better access to you at work than anyone else does.

- Make 'holes in your day' to get to their school for special events, *especially* if the kids realise you are missing out on something important at work.

- Phone or email the children from work with a brief message to let them know you are thinking of them.

- Involve the children in your working environment – take them there, introduce them to your colleagues.

- Tell the children about your work.

- Attend some of their school camps.

- Make sure you are available to them at crisis times – don't leave all that to their mother.

- Do regular canteen duty at school.

- Pick them up from school when you can.

IDEA FOR ACTION:

Pick one of these things to do each week and schedule it in your diary.

I know that Dad makes his best effort to be a good dad, and that when he comes home he is full-on as a dad and doesn't bring his work stresses home. When he comes in from work he wants to know about my day and helps me with my homework. Even if he can't help he makes it clear when he will be able to help. What's not so good sometimes is that occasionally Dad has to work really hard. Then when he gets home it gets to him and it gets to everyone else. When it spills out like that, then I realise what he is doing with us the rest of the time.

Naomi Creelman

I f there is one thing I would do differently it would be to get a regular meal time for the children. We have too many meals on stools around the kitchen table and we only have dinner together about three times a week maximum. Although we do a huge amount together as a family at other times, I think a regular mealtime together would be one change I'd make.

Neale Fong

chapter 4

Make time for kids – on weeknights

When Dad walks in the door everyone yells and runs to him because we know he is going to play or tackle us, or even just cook dinner with us.

Jessica Anderson

Do you find coming home from work both a pleasure and a tough time? Do you wish you could avoid this most difficult time of day?

The first twenty minutes after arriving home from work is, everyone agrees, the toughest part of the day for everyone in the family. The biology underlying the deficiency of brain chemicals that occurs after busy days and causes tiredness is discussed later. The point is, children, mums and dads are all likely to be irritable, because they are all tired.

There is no doubt that some fathers who are aware of the chaos that occurs in the house at the end of the day around meal times deliberately find work to do or pretend they are working so that they don't arrive home at that time of day. You need to be honest with yourself. That's the time when your partner really needs you to be there, and it can be a very special time with the children if it is managed well.

When the kids were young I used to try and get home as often as possible at a reasonable hour, trying to leave around 5 p.m. A workmate who had six children used to come in my office around 5 p.m. at night just for a chat. He didn't have anything to do but he didn't want to get home at that chaotic time of day. I told him I wasn't going to hang around. I preferred to be at home. Anonymous, scientist

Do something special with the children at the end of the day.

I take the kids down to the beach in the evenings after work about three times a week. We drive down, buy a drink and park. We either just sit there and talk or we walk along the cliff or along the beach watching the windsurfers. I love teaching them to appreciate the beauty of the beach and the open air. It also helps me unwind after work. It gives me a great chance to talk to them. It would not have worked so well at home – they might be distracted by TV. I ask the kids how their day was. It is a good time to talk but sometimes they don't want to talk so we don't. Anyone can do it – it is easy and it is free (apart from the cost of the odd soft drink!)

Ken Watt

My father would do a really hard day's fencing in the days when there were no posthole diggers and any hole had to be dug with a crowbar and shovel, then ride home and be greeted by me demanding that he come and bowl to me in the backyard. That would release my mother from the task. But it never occurred to me then that my father might have been tired and would have preferred a rest and a cool drink.

Donald Bradman

Choose to coach one of your children's sporting teams as a means of ensuring that you spend this part of the day with them on at least one day of the week.

One way that I make sure I get time with my kids during the week is to be the coach of one of their teams. That way I have to be there during the week for practice and every Saturday for the game. It is written into my schedule that at 3.30 every Wednesday I leave – no work, no meetings, no operations, nothing can be booked into that slot.

David Wood

Dinner time

I was listening to the radio in the car last night and the speaker talked about some recent research that showed that children who had the evening meal with their families at least 3–4 times a week were less likely to become drug addicts. Of course it is obvious that it is not the actual evening meal that protects them, nor just the content of the conversations around the evening meal. It is likely to be related to what the presence of the whole family around the meal table signifies: that the family believes it is important to do things together; that the family unit has some special significance; and that the children, as part of that unit, have a special place.

I grew up in a working class suburb. Lots of drinking, fast cars, girls and stealing. I did a bit of all of that too, but the main thing that stopped me getting into trouble bigtime was the knowledge that if I was caught it would let my family down and break my dad's heart.

Anonymous, carpenter

The family evening meal is not the only way of doing things together. If you can't eat together with your children in the evenings, you can certainly find other ways to do things together; but the majority of the fathers interviewed stressed the importance of that meal as a crucial part of their family life. It is potentially so important that I have included quite a range of expressed views about it:

■ The busier the family, the more important the family meal ritual can become

I believe family rituals are important. Sunday is our special family day. John cooks everyone breakfast and we have a family dinner together. We try to have a family activity or outing that we all choose together. This helps the children know how important they are to us – that they count to us, they are special. One of the important things about this ritual is that it creates order, a reliable pattern, within the chaos of busy lives.

Julia Anderson

■ Try to have dinner with the family at least 2–3 times every week

My high points with the kids were not so much the sport or speech nights when they won awards and praise from their peers, but all those occasions when we are just sitting at the table in the evening with the family together being happy. (As we spoke, Daniel and Georgia were doing the washing up behind us and laughing and joking with each other. He quietly pointed over his shoulder and nodded and said, 'That's what I mean – when the kids are happy in the family.')

Jim McCluskey

The only other thing we do on a daily basis is to make sure that we always eat together every night of the week. I don't want to make it sound idyllic, because we often end up fighting, but it is important to us.   Ian Frazer

As a kid, we always had dinner together at 7 o'clock with my two sisters and brothers and we all talked a lot.   Geoff Marsh

Having dinner with your family can be done if you remain flexible

We have always eaten together. Meal times have always been organised around my cricket schedule. Rather than having a drink with the players after practice, I would usually come home so I could have a meal with the family. During our meals we have always talked a lot and never watched TV, then when they were young I used to read them stories every night after dinner.   John Inverarity

Having a family meal has been difficult because of my long working hours as a cardiothoracic surgeon, but we have tried to do it 2–3 times a week.   Mark Edwards

Monday to Friday is hard, being a neurosurgeon. I try to get home at least one night a week for the evening meal and usually on the weekends, but lately I have been working all of Saturday and working late every night. It is hard in neurosurgery when you are presented with urgent cases of patients with brain tumours – they cannot really wait.   Paul Bannan

You can choose to make it a priority

Our evening meal was really important to us. We would always sit around and talk. I chose to avoid a lot of evening activities when the kids were younger so I didn't cut into family time.   Ray Arthur

I had a really difficult lifestyle till I was about 40 – I was on the road a lot and late at home a lot. It was a period of rapid growth in my work. I made a few decisions, though, to try to spend more time with the children.

I decided to try to be home for dinner every night at 6.30 p.m., and unless there is an evening meeting, I have been pretty good at doing that. Lately that has not happened because I guess the children are older and have their own lifestyles. Only two of them live at home anyway. Now we have Monday nights at home as a designated family tea night.

                                                          Michael Chaney

■ Some dads always find it hard

By the time I get home the kids are always getting ready to go to bed. I seldom have an evening meal with the children, I guess partly because the younger ones cannot wait until I get home. I typically eat by myself, usually after the children are in bed. We do a special family meal on weekends to try to make up for that. Glen Begley

Both my wife and I work, so we tend to eat late and the kids don't always eat with us. It is hard to structure eating dinner with them into our day. Anonymous, doctor

■ Time together over an evening meal isn't always the best choice

We always had the evening meals together although it wasn't the interaction point – there were lots of other points that were probably more significant, especially the period between meal time and bedtime. Allan Chapple

■ If you can't do dinner, perhaps lunch is an option for you when the children are home

Dad often came home at lunchtime when we were younger and I clearly remember him lying on the floor listening to the news at lunchtime with me lying next to him using his tummy as a pillow. Jane Perkins

■ Going out for dinner every week is another option

Dinner together has not been a big thing for us as a family. I guess it's partly because we eat out frequently. Because I work on weekends, Monday and Tuesday evenings are my 'weekend', so we go out and eat on those nights, and I think they are our special family dinner time. Dennis Cometti

▨ Stimulate discussion around the table

There are crucial times in the day, either before the kids go to school or dinner time, when you can connect with them and find out what's going on. In our house we found dinner time to be a good space at home to talk, have dinner, watch the news together and discuss it.   Geoff Gallop

Meal times were special at home. Dad was always there. Dad always tried to be there, and as we grew up he used meal times as an opportunity to develop our thinking skills — he used to often raise an issue and deliberately take the opposite side to the position we would take, simply to get us thinking and working out our own position.   Jane Perkins

▨ Turn the TV off or sell it

In terms of family time, for many years we didn't have a TV set — we used to hire one in the school holidays only. Most of the time we talked or played chess.   Ian Constable

During our meals we have always talked a lot and never watched TV.
    John Inverarity

▨ Get an answering machine, at least for meal times

When my family and I first started going over to my brother's house for dinner after he became a parish minister, it was always a nightmare because he was telephoned at least three or four times during dinner. I knew those who were calling were in need, but I still found it annoying. Why should the person on the end of the phone have the right to interrupt us, I selfishly thought? Then one night I noticed something different. We had a peaceful, lovely evening talking as a family, undisturbed. Then he told me what he had done. He had bought an answering machine. I was so impressed I did the same thing. Now we rarely answer calls between 6 p.m. and 8 p.m. in the evening. I can have dinner with the kids and read them stories uninterrupted.

▨ It is important to listen to your children's stories at dinner time

Many of those interviewed described how their mother heard about their day's activities but their father didn't seem as interested or 'tuned in'. This occurred whether the parents lived together or separately. Dinner time provides another opportunity for fathers to actually listen to what is happening in their children's lives.

We always ate together, and at the meal time there was a lot of competition for getting a word in. It was not a strict meal time, though, because there were six children and often, some would not be there, but nevertheless, we sat around listening to each other's news and stories.

Jock Clough

Dinner is very important in our family. We will even make dinner later if necessary so that we can all eat together. We have never had TV, although we did borrow one for the Olympics, but then we gave it back when they were over. During dinner I usually start with one child and ask that person to tell us all about their day. That way they all get to have a go at being focused on either once in three days or more often. Of course if they don't want to talk about that day we let them pass.

Geoff Creelman

▦ Try cooking one special meal a week/month

If you and your partner both work, share the cooking load and avoid the traditional stereotypes.

▦ Find reasons for celebration during some evening meals

In our family as the children grew up we had a tradition of celebrating anything good that happened to one of them. Whether it was a school report, merit certificate, runs at cricket, joining the school band or anything really, we would have a celebration at the meal table. One of the children would have to stand up and propose a toast and make a small speech. Later as they got older we kept a bottle of champagne in the fridge for such occasions. It was done semi-seriously and the kids all learnt to be able to give praise and to speak in front of others.

Ian Brayshaw

One of the best things we have done as parents is to make a big deal about always celebrating their achievements. If there isn't an obvious reason to have a celebration then we invent one.

Ken McAullay

▦ After dinner, go back to work if you need to

I always come home for dinner and I put the kids to bed. If I've got more work to do then I'll go back to the office afterwards rather than miss that family time.

Tim Willoughby

I never changed nappies (I'm from a different generation), but I made sure that I came home so we always had dinner together, even if it meant that I went back to the lab later on when they were in bed. Gus Nossal

■ Work with your partner to create surprises that are fun

It is easy for the homes of busy people to be serious places, lacking in spontaneous fun and humour. Of course our brain is just another organ and it can get exhausted, like overworked muscles. Think of some fun things you can do with your children in the evening. Of course you need to check that your idea is not going to prevent them from finishing an important assignment at school, so be careful about the surprise element. It might be an hour of board games, a sudden trip to the movies or the beach, a family sleepover night (everyone sleeping on mattresses on the living room floor in front of the fire with marshmallows), a game in the yard in the dark, sparklers on the lawn, a water fight, a family album or slide night with hot chocolate, etc.

Spontaneity and surprise are important. Do the unexpected. Occasionally, when it's time to go to bed, we'll take the kids in their pyjamas and race off and get an ice cream. When I get home from work sometimes we just jump in the car and head off to Fremantle or Kings Park, sometimes to the movies. It is the break from routine that keeps life interesting. Occasionally, I will grab some sparklers and we will head out to the back lawn and act like idiots. In fact it's these moments of unpredictable silliness which are especially important in the kids' lives. We did the sparkler thing out in the desert on one of our trips and the little ones often talk about it. The little one calls them 'splarkers' and it's now a regular call at any off-beat moment, almost a code word for 'fun'. Tim Willoughby

One of the nicest things about Dennis is his sense of humour. We have a lot of laughs at home. We never had humour when I was a kid with my dad. He was very serious. But our house has been full of laughter.
Velia Cometti

Switch your focus from work to kids

Busy people often bring home their work inside their heads. The busier you are the more likely it is for this to happen. Your brain will continue to turn things over long after you have left the workplace. In order to avoid the problem of not really being 'present' to your children, you need to work hard at switching off your work thoughts and focusing on your children.

Often I was physically present but mentally absent. My work was 'thinking intensive' and I always felt I was always responsible for planning, leading and conducting activities, even in my head at night. It's easy for that sort of stuff to keep going on between the ears when you get home.

Allan Chapple

Kids need their dad to be able to focus on them. Dad must be able to switch off when he gets home from work. I find that if I'm under a lot of pressure at work I sometimes can't switch off. That's mostly during the week. On Monday and Tuesday, after my working weekend, I'm pretty relaxed because there is not much that can 'come back and bite me' on those days. Weekends, when you finish your job, you've finished, and you get closure on that part of your life until the next weekend.

Dennis Cometti

You just have to be flexible so that when they want to talk to you you are willing to do so. I always just put aside what I'm doing and talk to them. Sometimes they would come in and sit on the bed and talk late at night. Of course sometimes it's impossible – if I'm in Question Time or in the middle of a speech. I guess it is similar to a surgeon operating on somebody – you can't interrupt then – but beyond that you should never be too busy to talk to your family. That's really what it boils down to. It's not a terribly revolutionary theory but it seems common sense to me that if you want to tell your children that they are important the best way of doing it is to never be too busy when they want to talk to you.

John Howard

What happens when you can't turn your work off

I didn't have good strategies for dealing with pressure and switching off. I've learnt from my mistakes, but unfortunately in the middle period of the kids' childhood I wasn't able to focus enough. Allan Chapple

When dads are mentally detached from their kids, for long periods, life at home has no laughter and fun. Then there is a short burst of humour, joking and fun, but it doesn't last. Ian Robinson

When I was Mayor of St Kilda it was hard to be present to the kids emotionally because I was always being called on the telephone or on my mobile. It was my first occasion of being in the public eye and I didn't have the wisdom to turn the phone off very often. Tim Costello

■ **Failing to focus on your children when you are home can make them feel that you don't really care about them**

Dad was away almost all the time working for main roads. When he was home he was emotionally absent. Better that he wasn't there, really.

Anonymous psychologist

Being flexible

■ **If you work in bursts, use the 'change the shape of your time' strategy**

Some jobs inevitably have bursts of time where frantic activity and long hours can't be avoided – construction deadlines, research grant applications, accounting deadlines, sporting fixtures, preparations for big shows or expositions, writing books (like this one) and so on. It is unrealistic to suggest that you don't have to work extra hours around those times.

What is possible, though, is to change the shape of the year in the same way that we discussed changing the shape of your day: work in a burst for that period of time but then make it up to your family by shortening your hours after that burst. When you are working in bursts it's very helpful to make a promise to the family that you will do something special with them when it's all over. Make sure that you keep your promise.

My worst time occurred when I was finishing my thesis. I was working ten to twelve hours a day for about nine months. It was terrible. But it was a time that just had to be endured – there was no option.   Allan Chapple

When I was doing my doctorate, I had to work long hours and, when it was coming to its conclusion, the hours were even longer because I had to finish it in America and then head back to Australia. I promised the family that I would take some time off when I finished, to make up for the long hours I had worked. I love my work and was tempted to rush off and start my new job, but when my doctorate was finished I kept that promise and we travelled across the United States in our camper van for a couple of months. We stayed in national parks, camping by glaciers and mountain lakes. It turned out to be one of the finest trips I've ever done with the family. Any work I might have done in those months would have long ago faded from my memory and from significance, but the memory of the pleasure, beauty and peace of that trip will stay with me forever.

■ **If you are really busy during the week, make weekends a mini vacation**

Some people make an effort to go away on weekends if they are really busy during the week and don't spend much of the time with their family. This can create a real mini vacation in the absence of much togetherness during the week.

As a young father I was Dean of St John's College in the University of Queensland, and had to dine with the students between Monday and Thursday. It was a very formal affair, all male and all gowned. On Fridays, however, we would pick the children up and head off to the beach and get fish and chips or pizza on the way. We'd muck around in the car, playing games or singing. We discovered Elgar and Neil Diamond on those trips. I saw them as 'mini holidays' at the end of every week. It wouldn't have been the same if we'd stayed at home.   Peter Carnley

■ **If your weekends are busy, create 'weekends' during the week**

Because of my job in the media, particularly with Channel Seven during the football season, weekends have always been the most intense period of work for me, and I have to travel a lot. My two children have never known anything else, so they've just accepted it. What I do, though, is try to make up for it during the week.   Dennis Cometti

I've always been very busy in my work. I had Friday and Saturday off and I defended that mercilessly, although to be perfectly honest that's more the case now – I was never as good as I should have been when the children were young.   Peter Carnley

Summary

- The first twenty minutes after arriving home from work is the toughest time of day. Are you avoiding it?

- Have some evening meals with the family each week.

- Even if making time to have dinner with the family is very difficult, if you remain flexible you can do it: you can choose to make it a priority.

- Not everyone finds that time together over an evening meal is the best choice: perhaps lunch is an option when the children are home, or going out for dinner once a week.

- Stimulate discussion around the table.

- Listen to your children's stories at dinner time.

- Try taking the responsibility for cooking one special meal a week/month, depending on your circumstances.

- Come home for dinner, then return to work if you need to.

- Create celebrations.

- Invent fun things in the evening together – don't make home too serious a place.

- Work hard at switching off your work thoughts and focusing on your children when you are home for dinner.

- If you work in bursts, use the 'change the shape of your time' strategy.

- If you are really busy during the week, make weekends a mini vacation.

- If your weekends are always busy with work, create 'weekends' during the week.

IDEA FOR ACTION:

Pick one of these things to do each week and schedule it in your diary.

When you talk about important things with the kids, try to make it natural and find a soft way to talk about it.

Allan Chapple

When we were really busy Dad would always think about us and he would take us out. For example during my exams he would come and get me and take me out for lunch.   Corinne Arthur

Be proactive

Fathering is like any other skill – no matter how much natural talent and intuition we have, if we are going to improve, we need to do some learning, and then evaluate our progress. As with other activities, to succeed we must also overcome any mental blocks we may have.

Here is a table comparing how we learn skills, evaluate progress and recognise blocks/problems in one work situation (computing) and one leisure example (golf) compared with our fathering. We need to learn to apply them to our fathering.

	Learning computing software	Improving at golf	Fathering
Planning	Ring computer consultant for advice	Ring golf shop for advice Book lessons	?
Learning skills	Manuals and courses	Lessons, books and videos	?
Cost	Time, hassle and cost of buying software and undergoing training	Lessons and video, plus twenty hours of leisure time	?
Evaluation	Being able to use the software effectively	Better golf scores	?
Maintaining benefits	Annual refresher course Talking with colleagues who use the same program	Regular practice Refresher lessons Competition	?

Many busy fathers are used to planning in this sort of way. They are also useful skills for fathering, and another example of how success at work can help make you a more effective father. Yet many of us resist the idea of applying these sorts of skills to fathering.

Becoming a more 'proactive' father

This chapter is about the first step in improving our fathering: planning. The focus is on being 'proactive', on working out what our children really need, and bearing these needs in mind when we are with them. We may need to do a little work, but that's exactly what we have to do for any project in our jobs. And while our children aren't 'work', they do deserve at least the same thought and effort that we are happy to put in for our jobs.

A lot of men don't think about fathering because men really don't like to think about the future. For example, they don't like to think about their own retirement or death, but if you say to them, 'what sort of lifestyle would your family have if you died?', then they have to start thinking about it – that's why we should all have enough life insurance. Men usually just want to wait and see what happens but you need to plan things in advance, at least to some extent, or you won't be able to do them.

David Pocock

It is helpful to have a strategy for good fathering. We need to know what to do for our children and we need to be able to work out whether we are succeeding as fathers before it is too late. Going back to the golf analogy, can you imagine trying to improve your golf without first accepting the need to plan a way to do it? Without a plan, how would you know where to turn, regardless of whether there were books, videos, lessons available?

What does being 'proactive' mean?

Busy career people often suffer the 'tyranny of the in-tray' (which now includes the email inbox), which means that they constantly function in reactive mode. They get little time to plan for the future because of the incessant demands of new problems, urgent deadlines and so on – the *urgent* can easily dominate the *important*. It is easy to father that way too, to react to problems that children have instead of planning ahead.

Let's look at the task of fathering, just for a moment, in the same way that you look at a task you might undertake at work. Instead of just 'going with the flow', and being reactive, what if you actually do some planning? Would it be worthwhile?

A lot of the fathers interviewed at first said that they hadn't put much planning into their fathering, but on further questioning it became clear that many of them had done so, without realising it. Even consciously waiting for 'teachable moments' generally meant they had an idea of what the children needed: values, someone to listen to their problems, someone to help them develop good learning skills and so on. Unfortunately, just waiting for these teachable moments will not always be enough.

No matter what the task, the likely outcome is much improved by having information and advice early on. Marriages are more likely to succeed if the couple undergoes marriage preparation, and discusses communication, sexuality, parenting, role models of husband/wife and the difficult times ahead, such as the arrival of a first baby, the seven-year itch, a mid-life crisis, and more. 'Forewarned is fore-armed.'

The same applies to the children's schooling – you are much more likely to be effective in helping them with their schoolwork if you understand exactly what it is they are going to be studying – what the course requirements are, what the goals of the course are, and how the students will be assessed.

Of course the ultimate example is our work. If I talk to the man who installs swimming pools about having a pool put into my back yard, I know that the first thing he will ask me is 'What do you want?' Then he will tell me whether or not it can be done, how much it will cost, what the local council regulations are, how he will ensure that it is safe and what maintenance will be needed to keep the pool functioning at its best. He will also then check on whether or not there are any sewerage pipes, underground septic tanks or other obstacles that would need to be dealt with. If he starts digging before he does this planning, clearly, he will run into problems.

The same applies to parenting. We will increase our effectiveness if we do the same thing: if we ask ourselves what the goals in fathering are, how we can best achieve them, what it will cost us, how we will know we have achieved these goals, how we will maintain the benefits, and how we will identify any blocks (in our own minds) to progress.

If this is a difficult concept, it might be helpful to think about doctors and heart disease: if doctors only *reacted* to problems, we would just treat patients who had already suffered a heart attack. Being *proactive* means we have worked hard to cut down people's fat intake, get them to exercise and quit smoking, get their blood pressure checked, and so on. That approach has dramatically cut down the rate of deaths from heart attacks and saved over a half a million lives in the world over the past twenty years.

The same goes for car accidents. If we only react to problems as they occur we will simply provide sophisticated emergency facilities and handle the victims as they pour in, something which I did a lot of as an intern. It was like a MASH tent some nights as drunken drivers would crash into each other all night and unseat-belted young women would come in having crashed through the windscreen, the broken glass shredding their beautiful faces. The new seat belt laws, Random Breath Testing and other proactive approaches have dramatically reduced that sort of casualty.

The same applies to work, of course – the man who fails to do any planning in his work is unlikely to succeed. Even the least organised person must learn to plan their day and not just wait for success to come marching through the door – it never comes. Being proactive works in health, at work, and in our fathering.

If your fathering is only reactive, your kids might miss out

If you remain a mostly reactive rather than proactive father, your children run the risk of missing out on some important things. They might miss out on certain bits of advice because that situation just didn't come up. Another problem with the reactive approach is that where there is more than one child in a family, the one with the most apparent needs can demand and may get more attention than other children. Quiet children might then miss out on their share of your attention. Being proactive means that these sorts of problems can be avoided.

Some of the interviewees felt very strongly that dads should spend more time thinking about what fathering is all about.

To young dads today I would say, don't just react to children's problems, but try to plan ahead. Fathers should focus on positive parenting. Don't just react to problems when they occur. Richard Court

I could have been more proactive in my fathering. I tended to be more reactive to the kids' problems. Ian Constable

(Liz: *No, Ian, that's just not true. Whenever there was a problem you didn't just sort out the problem, you worked out a strategy for the future as well.*)

I really admire Ian Constable for the way he has been so proactive in his fathering. He and Liz have thought it through a lot. Graham Barrett

I tend to be a spontaneous, reactive person rather than a proactive planner. I guess I am about half and half, when I think about it. I do tend

to think about what my kids could gain from particular activities and strategies and work it into my day sometimes. I think I could have improved in this area, though – I would like to have spent more time thinking strategically about each of the kids' future and working on it.

Peter Prout

The way Jan and I tend to be proactive is that we sit down and reflect together about these things. If we think something is missing in their life we work out what we need to do. Usually Jan spots it, but sometimes it's me.

Peter Newman

The idea of being proactive in fathering is something that a lot of successful men have not thought much about.

We have not spent a lot of time thinking about our parenting, and I guess we have just made these kinds of decisions on the run. In fact, it is only as you asked me now that I am really even thinking about it. I guess more will come to mind after we stop talking.

Wayne Cormack

If the children know you are proactive, that you are often thinking about them, about what they need and how they are, it can mean a lot to them.

I've never asked myself whether I was proactive or reactive with regard to the kids' learning. I guess I really should have asked that question of myself. I spent lots of time reading to them and encouraging them to take an interest in things. I guess now that you've got me thinking about it, I've mostly been reactive.

Allan Chapple

(Alison: *'Allan, I used to be really frustrated because I just couldn't get you to think about setting goals for your fathering.'*)

I remember my dad coming down to the school playground on cold winter days with some hot soup – it felt fantastic. We didn't have money to buy warm pies and things from the tuckshop so it was really special.

Marg Robinson

Sometimes this type of approach to fathering requires men to overcome a lot of internal resistance – they would rather 'go with the flow'. Dads who have plenty of time with their children find that they don't have to invent 'teachable moments'; enough of them arise in everyday life to allow them to teach their kids what they want them to know, provided they are open to taking these opportunities. What matters is deciding in advance what it is that your kids need and then using those moments, rather than letting them slip by. The proactive part is simply thinking in advance about what it is your children really need.

I think there are enough opportunities on the run for you to teach kids what you think is importants.   Brian Edwards

What are appropriate goals?

If you sit down and think about fathering, there is one crucial question you need to ask: 'What is the goal of my fathering?' This is no different from setting goals in work or sport – if you don't know where you are headed, how can you develop any strategy to get there?

I'm not really proactive with fathering but I would call myself an 'active opportunist'. I look for opportunities, and I think there are probably enough opportunities in a child's life to cover most of the required teaching moments. Of course that depends on whether you have the time available to be there when those teaching moments occur!   Kanishka Raffel

Thinking about what our children really need is crucial when we are thinking about a strategy for good fathering. If we don't set goals – goals related to what we most want for our children – we are likely to not achieve those things, and to allow ourselves to be distracted along the way. You can set achievement goals for your children – to become a doctor, to do an apprenticeship and get a trade, to live near you, to become a Test cricketer, for example – or you can focus on setting more generic goals.

I have quizzed a number of people and groups about what they think children really need. I have given them the following list of choices and said, 'If you could "wave your magic wand" and choose four of these outcomes, but only four, for your kids, which would you choose?' Here is the list:

- [ ] Lots of money
- [ ] A nice house
- [ ] Tallness
- [ ] A Jaguar and Mercedes Benz
- [ ] A lifelong love of learning
- [ ] A university degree
- [ ] A prestigious job
- [ ] Joy and happiness
- [ ] Sporting success
- [ ] Values of honesty, commitment and kindness
- [ ] Good health
- [ ] A partner
- [ ] Fame
- [ ] A beach cottage
- [ ] Religious beliefs similar to your own

Choose the four you would want for your children. Here are the choices of several groups of dads that were sampled. These choices were clearly ahead of the rest:

- [x] Values of honesty, commitment and kindness
- [x] Joy and happiness
- [x] Good health
- [x] A lifelong love of learning

When pushed about what children really needed most, the people interviewed obviously did not think of expensive educations, expensive houses (also known as big mortgages) or flash cars; they thought of values, happiness, health and a love of learning.

Having your goals clear in your mind is a good way to start setting your fathering priorities.

'I am too tired after work to think about fathering'

That's perfectly reasonable. Evenings after work are not the best time to sit down and talk about proactive fathering. Perhaps it would be easier to sit down and discuss your fathering plans on a weekend or some other time when you are not tired. This could be planned in advance, as a once a month thing, with your partner and/or with some mates.

Don't be *too obviously* proactive

When I talk about planning your fathering I am not talking about spending each day in a totally task-oriented way. The fathers I spoke to (and I myself) all felt the same way: it is helpful to identify these goals and keep them 'ticking over in the back of your mind', but you don't need to spend every waking moment agonising over them. You don't want to be 'in your children's face' about the goals whenever you're with them.

In fact if, when you spend time with your children, you are *obviously* trying to instruct them about some important issue that you have identified as a need in their lives, they will probably resist listening to you, particularly as they get older. If it is obvious that you have engineered the situation to give them a lecture, you've probably already lost them. Most fathers find it more productive to just make good use of the 'teachable moments'.

It's a bit like chairing a work meeting. If there is useful discussion occurring it's important not to stop it, but it's also important to keep the aim of the meeting in the back of your mind so that the goals are achieved.

I do think proactively about important things for the kids, but then I put it to the back of my mind. It's important not to have it too far in the front of your mind or you'll feel like you're imposing too much of your views on them.   Peter Newman

There are other reasons why it is not a good idea to be totally task-oriented in your activities with your children. Not only do children not enjoy it; dads don't enjoy it either, because it feels too much like hard work. Of course there are occasions when a structured discussion must take place. If your son has got into some trouble at school, for instance, when you come home, tell him that you have to talk it over with him, and that you want to make a time with him to do that. You might go out for a milkshake to talk about it, but there is a clear agenda, and your son knows he will have to deal with the issue. Other than a situation like that, I think a background agenda works best.

Of course the kids wouldn't see it as a strategic activity, as my plans would be hidden in the everyday activity.   Peter Prout

When my oldest son reached the legal drinking age of 18 he had great pleasure in inviting me that week to the pub for a beer. We went and played pool and had a couple of beers. He did something that helped me enormously that first night. He told me that he was happy to go out to the pub with me as long as I didn't behave like a parent, asking him about study, work, values, etc., but behaved with him like a mate. Since then I have steadfastly stuck to that rule, and it has turned out beautifully. I have plenty that I need to talk to him about, but there are lots of other opportunities to talk about important stuff. In the pub we talk about all sorts of stuff, mostly laughing with each other. I really enjoy it. To have a big tough 18-year-old want to be in a pub with his dad is about all I can ask for. He went overseas for a year, and when I went past that pub I missed him.

Summary

- It helps to have a strategy for fathering.

- Be 'proactive': plan what to say to your children rather than just reacting to problems when they occur. If you do your fathering only reactively, your children might miss out.

- No matter what the task, the likely outcome is improved by having information and advice early.

- Your children should know that you often think about them – about what they need and how they are.

- Part of being proactive is deciding on appropriate goals for your children.

- The top four wishes of other dads for their kids are:
  1 Values of honesty, commitment and kindness
  2 Joy and happiness
  3 Good health
  4 A lifelong love of learning

- Don't be so proactive that you are 'in their face' with goals and agendas.

IDEA FOR ACTION:

Think of how you can help your children achieve the four goals you wish for them.

Right... we've got 45 minutes of playtime. It may seem like a lot but that can easily be swallowed by administration. So I'll keep this short...

Focusing on being a good dad has helped me understand the pressures that other dads are under. It has also helped to make me a more balanced person. I am a fairly 'driven' person so if I didn't have family I think I'd become absolutely obsessed with work. I'm already described as being fairly driven so it is likely that I would focus on work to the exclusion of other things. I'd be driven in just one direction. Family is, and should be, the ultimate balance.

John Dickson

Being a dad has helped me know how to deal with the apprentices at work.

Graham Smith

Chapter 6

How good fathering improves dad's productivity at work

Good fathering will make you more productive and successful at work

Fathers who are confident about their children worry less, have a more relaxed view of life and consequently are more likely to be healthy and productive at work.

I also know when I go to bed every night that I have truly tried my best to be a good employee, father, spouse and member of the community. On some days one of these groups will get let down, but on balance I know that I am trying my best and at the end of the day that is all anyone can expect. Daniel Petre

Also, I have found, as have others, that learning about parenting provides excellent skills for managing staff (although I never let on to them that my management techniques come from classes on management of children!). This is because people skills are largely the same for children as for adults.

The fact that committed fathers can be just as successful as anyone else in the workplace is not widely known. It does take longer to reach the same career level as a workaholic, but there is not the huge trade-off that many imagine. A recent study from Emory University in the United States, conducted over 40 years, showed that fathers who were involved with their children may have slightly delayed success in their career compared with those who were not involved, but in the long run they went just as far in their work. This study particularly applied to fathers who were involved in their children's mental development and their adolescent social development.

When I asked the men interviewed if their productivity would have been altered had they chosen to overwork rather than spend time with their families, they gave amazing answers. They said that their productivity *rose* because they chose to spend less time at work and more with their children – they estimated the amount to be between 15 and 40 percent, with an average of 26 percent. If this held true for every working man in Australia, the increased productivity that would ensue if just one in every ten fathers altered their working lives to focus more on their children would be worth another $4.6 billion to the country's economy.

I've always had trouble establishing the boundary between work and family. If I didn't have the kids I would just keep working at night and over the weekends and I would end up getting staler and staler. But I don't have to force myself to be with the kids; I look forward to it, and I prefer it. It's just that I'm not strong enough to stop working. It has been great for me because I go back to work refreshed, so work benefits a lot from my fathering.

Peter Newman

Am I more productive at work because of my commitment to fathering? Absolutely. I am much more productive. That's because being away from work and spending time with the family helps me to focus on goals and evaluate the resources available and cut out all the peripheral crap and stupid meetings that don't achieve anything. It stops me reading reports that I don't need to read and basically helps me to cull out the stuff that's a waste of time.

Daniel Petre

This has been the observation of many of the fathers in these interviews. By getting out of the 'goldfish bowl' of work, they felt they had been able to be more objective about their work and put it in context. Also, they were better able to handle their staff because of what they'd learnt through parenting teenagers and because of what they'd learnt from books about how to actively listen and how to really focus on people when you talk to them.

If you have a good relationship with your children it is easier to be emotionally committed to work. Those who don't relate to their kids can't make this emotional commitment to work. I have no doubt that if I had endless trouble with my children and I was fighting with them all the time I don't think I could do my job nearly as well.

John Howard

The idea that employers should encourage their workers to be better family men and women is fairly new – until recently work and family were always seen as in conflict with each other. This potential flow of benefits from work to fathering and back again is illustrated in the following figure:

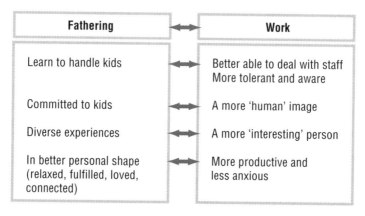

Fathering		Work
Learn to handle kids	↔	Better able to deal with staff More tolerant and aware
Committed to kids	↔	A more 'human' image
Diverse experiences	↔	A more 'interesting' person
In better personal shape (relaxed, fulfilled, loved, connected)	↔	More productive and less anxious

Bosses: notice the arrows go both ways.

Women, particularly in male-dominated workplaces, still often get the 'You will just have to choose – family or work' line. Now men, as they start taking their fathering seriously, are beginning to get it, too.

I think it is time bosses realised that if they encourage their workers who are fathers to be better fathers, they will actually get improved productivity in the workplace. Why is this? It is simple, really. Firstly, dads learn a lot from fathering that can be useful in the workplace. Secondly, and equally importantly, dads benefit so much from being involved with their children that they are less stressed, more relaxed and better able to work efficiently and productively.

Here are some of the specific benefits that fathering can bring.

■ You learn how to deal with people

Learning how to manage children often covers the necessary ingredients for managing conflict and personality differences at work.

As a cleaner at a school the kids come up and talk to me a lot. Because I am a dad I can understand and respect what they are talking about. Otherwise I might just get short-fused with them. These kids see me everywhere around town and always talk to me.   Greg Wade

Being a dad has helped me to learn to trust my intuition. That's really what fathering is about because it's hard to be prescriptive about it. I take that style with me when I go to work.   Tony Cooke

Fathering has helped my work a lot. I think it has made me more patient (you can't try to apply logic to a two-year-old and lose patience when they can't follow your line of reasoning). Also, I have learnt to communicate at someone else's level. In the workplace it is really important to communicate at different levels, and kids can teach you that.   Daniel Petre

You develop a more 'human' image in your workplace

The more involved you are with your children's lives – leaving work to attend special functions, having photographs of the children at work, letting the children telephone you at various times, and so on – the more people at work will realise that you're a human being. That ought to help in your relationships with them.

You are out of the goldfish bowl

Small personality differences and difficulties can appear much larger in the small goldfish bowl of the workplace. Getting out of the workplace and out of work mode to spend time with children, particularly if you take them away with you on camping trips, for example, enables you to come back to work and see it in its true perspective.

You become a more interesting person

It is so boring at work or social functions when people talk only about work. Parents like to be asked about their children, especially if they know that the person asking has a genuine regard for their children or for parenting in general. If you're a committed dad you're much more likely to ask others about their children – they may love to tell you.

▪ You avoid becoming stale

If you work too little you are unproductive and unfulfilled. The right amount and you are productive, enjoy it, are fulfilled and have a balanced life. Too much and your productivity falls off, even if you're putting in more hours. You get stale and grumpy. This point is illustrated in the following figure, the 'overwork reduces productivity' bell curve.

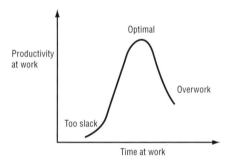

The reason for this curve is that the brain cells and their connections function by releasing small chemicals, neurotransmitters, all the time. When your brain is very active, lots of neurotransmitters are released and, not surprisingly, you can run short of them. When these chemicals are depleted you start to lose efficiency and make mistakes. The trend should be to send the workaholics home before they burn out!

In the 'bad old days' of medicine we used to work for two to three days in a row without any sleep. That was dangerous, because our brains' chemical stores of neurotransmitters became depleted. They don't ask young doctors to work those sorts of hours any more and nor should they. Would you like to be looked after by a junior doctor who hasn't slept for two days? Overwork reduces efficiency and makes it more likely that you will make a significant mistake.

Overwork definitely reduces productivity, whereas if my workers 'get a life' I think it definitely helps productivity. I employ over 250 staff and am responsible for about another 2,500 contractors, and I can tell you they are no more productive for the extra time they work. Warren Reynolds

▦ Your work skills may improve

As a radio interviewer I improved my interviewing technique by virtue of my fathering. I no longer became nervous when interviewing the Prime Minister because I'd learnt to face a more harrowing assault from the 'why' brigade at home.
Liam Bartlett

▦ You become more aware of what is happening in the lives of your staff

I think being a father is really helpful to my work. It has made me more sensitive to the needs of my staff and how they relate to their own families. My work has helped me to be able to give advice to people about the balance they achieve between their work and their home life. If I weren't a father I wouldn't be able to give that advice.
Warren Reynolds

▦ You may be able to help staff members who have difficult family issues to deal with

My fathering has helped me realise and understand problems that blokes have at work – problems that often arise from their home life. For example, one guy blames work for problems he is having at home but I know it's the other way around: it's his home life that's creating problems at work and causing him to work late.
Warren Reynolds

▦ You develop more tolerance

My children have given me a stronger sense of the world around me and a more defined social conscience. I'd like to think they'd also made me a more tolerant, less impatient person.
Liam Bartlett

Committed dads benefit personally and in their work

One of the most fascinating things about good fathering is that you can do it for selfish motives. I don't mean just the selfish motive of fulfilling your urge to love your children. I mean there are tangible benefits that flow from good fathering. And then work benefits because dads benefit.

The personal benefits

The benefits of fathering might seem intangible to some people but they rank as the most important to many dads. Here is a selection:

The children can stay emotionally close to you as they get older, if you are close to them

Since the boys have left school Ian is more their friend than their dad, although I am still their mother.   Liz Constable

Our three children gave us a huge amount of pleasure and joy. They didn't give us too many problems. Seeing them grow up, seeing where they are now, gives me a great sense of satisfaction. They've grown up level-headed and have met very nice partners. I love being around them. I really do like being around them. I work with the two boys. Suzie's not here and lives in Melbourne, which is great for her but it's a bit of a shame for me. Really I talk to the kids like friends, not as children.   Brian Edwards

I guess partly because I was a single parent for so many years I am close to my children. My son lives in Melbourne and our daughter is studying at the Academy of Performing Arts in Western Australia. She is very creative, artistic and a free spirit. It's taken her a while to find her niche but she's found it through music and performing arts. I am really proud of my son's independence. He went out straight after school and got a job, did tennis coaching and then took mature age exams for university entrance and has completed a degree in his late twenties. He has a good job now working in Melbourne in banking, and I have no hesitation in ringing him for my own personal financial advice. I love being able to do that.   Richard Court

I realised that I needed to be more of a friend than a replacement dad to my stepdaughters – they have their biological dads already. With each of them they have issues, of course, but I need to be their friend. I need to be able to draw alongside them as a friend – that's much more important. I think that this is probably a wise approach to use with my son Willem also. While I am his parent, his protector, provider, adviser and servant, I always want to walk beside him as a friend, his buddy.   Peter de Blanc

■ You relax into the greatest pleasures that life can give

Fathers should recognise that fathering provides the most enduring pleasure and the most enduring rewards, other than love for your wife. The

rest is just play-acting. Hobbies will never do it for you, nor will work. Make fathering your passion outside your work, because it will be a rich reward for you for the rest of your life. Ian Constable

I love being a dad. I really do. I knew I'd love it and I do.
Kanishka Raffel

One of the things I like about parenting is that it produces a nice little twist in life: that is, you put a lot of effort in but you get huge satisfaction back from your children as they mature into adults. Richard Court

My kids are the best gift I ever had. The days of each of their births are the best days of my life, ahead of grand finals and any medical successes. All I can think of when I think of them is joy and happiness and laughter. Of course they could remember times when Dad went crook at them, but I can't remember, myself. I just remember the times when they were kids and their little arms wrapped themselves around my neck, their smiling laughing faces, their senses of humour (each of them) and our thousands of hours of playing and mucking around. As older kids, things haven't changed. Many is the time I would like to have hugged the big boys when they were frightened of something, but they wouldn't have liked that, and they have to deal with things themselves now anyway. Such wonderful people, each of them. Full of life, kindness, warmth, love, humour and talent, each in their own way. Enough of that. Author, diary extract, 1997

No, there is not a lot that I think I'd do over again. It probably sounds like a terrible thing to say, but I don't actually regret anything that I've done with the children. As far as I can see I haven't left anything out. I was always there for them. Actually, to be perfectly honest, I think it was as much for me as for them. They were my lifeline – in some ways I was more dependent on them than they were on me. They were the family I never had. Brian Edwards

Being Premier of the state is hard work, but without a doubt the hardest thing I've ever done in my life is parenting. But seeing them now makes it all worthwhile. We are very close. Richard Court (in 2000)

I guess I would like my kids to know that I love them, of course, but also that I have a deep interest in them as people. I would like them to know what a richness they have brought to our lives and how grateful I am to

them for that richness. I have enjoyed grasping every opportunity I had to nurture them and I have loved having that responsibility.

John Inverarity

I'd like my kids to know that I've really enjoyed being a dad, more than anything else in my life. In fact the truth is, I don't want them to leave home. I'm already feeling a bit sad at the prospect. I remember once when I was sitting on a plane, ready to fly overseas to a conference, I was pondering about the fact that my eldest son was fifteen and one day he would leave home, and I just found myself crying, just sitting there in the plane.

Peter Le Soeuf

My three children are wonderful kids. Absolutely wonderful. It's a privilege to be with them, they are three of the best and they have given us a life that is very privileged. Anyone who looks at parenting as a chore is missing the experience. They give you so much pleasure, so much joy, and so much richness. These relationships are priceless. I have a strong sense of fathering being a gift. It is a gift that is given; I haven't created it.

Peter Newman

I get much more out of my relationship with my children than they ever get from me.

Kim Beazley

I would like the kids to know that they are the four most precious boys that ever existed, and that despite all my mistakes as a parent, I always believed they were capable of achieving their dreams. I will always be proud of them as people and whatever it is they accomplish. They have already brought enormous happiness to me in life, so whatever happens in the future, nothing would change the richness of the experience that I have had already with them. If people said to me, 'what's the best age for the children?' I would tell them I do not know yet – when they were young, I thought that was terrific, and as they get older, I think that is better, and then they get to be teenagers and young adults and I think it is better and better.

Glenn Begley

I would like them to know that fathering my three girls has been the richest thing I have ever done. All of the richest experiences I have had in my life have been around being a father. Also, I have gained so much in my own life from my children, as they have reciprocated my love in so many ways.

Peter Prout

I'd like the kids to know that I'd always looked forward to being a father. I don't know why. I was absolutely thrilled with them. I've loved them hugely from the moment of their birth. I can see all kinds of ways now that I wasn't as good a father as I wanted to be. There's lots of things I'd do differently if I could – but on the other hand I did mostly the best I knew at the time. I wanted to make sure that their childhood filled their memories with good things – lots of enjoyable and worthwhile experiences. My greatest desire for them was to know God for themselves, because I feel that knowledge about God is the best thing I could have given them. Oh, one last thing. I hope they realise what a wonderful mother they have. Allan Chapple

I don't think I'm a good dad. I'm away 70 to 90 percent of the time. My kids have turned out really well, but that's probably largely because of their mother. It is me who has missed out. Now I've got a grandchild and I just love spending time with him, and I realise what I've missed out on. I plan to change my current job so that I can work from home and I will not have to travel so much. That way I can be involved in my grandchild's upbringing. I can't wait to teach him how to ride a motorbike. Warren Reynolds

You will have more meaning in your life

For virtually everybody, their children's wellbeing is really more important than any success at work. If you could be guaranteed that trading off a bit of extra success at work would improve the mental, physical, emotional and spiritual wellbeing of your children, would you make the trade?

Committing to good fathering is an act of trust based on statistics and on understanding the important factors in children's upbringing. Knowing that your good fathering is likely to be effective can provide a deep sense of meaning and achievement in your life.

You will know love and acceptance yourself

There will be no uncertainty about the fact that when you give love you get love back. Many fathers who are absent from the fathering process are never quite sure whether their children really love them or just talk to them out of a sense of duty, as they would relate to the school principal.

Each of them has expressed love for me at various times, and often this has been my greatest tonic in life. I pray that they will be as fortunate as me in having a family with so much shared love and rich experiences.

Peter Prout

By knowing that the important things in life are taken care of, you can relax more. Knowing that you will be surrounded by a loving family network during your later years, no matter where they live, can generate a sense of emotional security for you.

▪ You may rediscover how to play

Being a parent is a roller-coaster ride, but it is fun. Kids make their fathers back into kids again.

Peter Newman

Play is more than just non-work. It is one of the pieces in the puzzle of our existence, a place for our excesses and exuberances. It is where life is lived in a very special way. It is a time when we forget our problems for a while and remember who we are. Play is more than just a game. It is where you recognise again the supreme importance of life itself. Like a child, you see life as it is and as it was meant to be. In play you can abandon yourself, you can immerse yourself without restraint, you can pierce life's complexities and confusions. You can be whole again, without trying.

Tim Hansell

▪ You will have rich memories

When I think about it, the ten best days of my life are all with the kids, and all something to do with nature, being out in the bush with them.

Peter Le Soeuf

▪ Your children keep you on a learning curve

Another benefit I get from having the kids is that they teach me a lot. Kids have got such a simple philosophy of life: they tell you what's important and what's not important. It's like the Bible says, 'Unless you become like a child ... ' – that means simplicity. I need to be reminded of it and kids do that.

Peter Newman

▪ Your children keep you connected to your community

Another advantage I get from having kids is that they get me out into the community and to sporting events. We have recently been going to watch the Dockers as season ticket holders, and that's because of Sam, our nine-year-old. We all go by train and I love it, but we wouldn't be going except for Sam. I'd probably be at home writing a paper about the role of community sports activities in a city's culture! The kids have also drawn me into the community of Fremantle. Through their friends, parents and other activities I have become much more a member of the community than I would otherwise have been.

Peter Newman

How good fathering automatically benefits your work

The evidence shows that:

- Committed fathers are healthier because they are more relaxed, more likely to have fun, less likely to overwork and more likely to take a bit of time off. Committed fathers have a lower incidence of hypertension and peptic ulcer, for example.
- Committed fathers are happier and less likely to be influenced by the stresses of work.
- Your 'treasure chest of memories and experiences' is full, and because you know it is full and can be drawn on at any time, you can relax – it's like knowing you have money in the bank to spend when you need to.
- If you are told you are going to die, you're not going to be plunged into a situation where you realise you have failed to spend enough time with your children
- You will have a better sex life with your partner. That's because your relationship will be better and your partner will be less frustrated with you and the children. You're taking your share of the parenting load, fulfilling your role as a father.

In the past I have been the classic overworking idiot who has worked so hard that when he goes on holidays it takes him three weeks to relax, and then he goes down with the 'flu. That doesn't happen to me now.

Daniel Petre

Counting the cost

If you don't sit down and ask yourself what the cost of trying the things suggested in this book will be, you could fail. No-one should ever start a project without first counting the cost, and I'm talking here about several kinds of cost: time, energy, money, at the very least.

My observation as a doctor is that people are likely to fail in their life tasks if they don't first count the cost, if they don't make the mental connection between the outcome and the cost. For example, people who are overweight need to go on a diet – they need to clearly visualise the cost in terms of hunger, food choices and lifestyle modifications. Similarly, cigarette smokers who want to quit smoking need to begin by acknowledging to themselves that it is going to be very tough and that they are going to feel uncomfortable – it won't be easy.

It's the same with being a father. You probably have to accept that some sort of sacrifice is needed.

Some of my decisions to sacrifice work for the children have cost money, but that is not a big deal. I am paid well enough and anyway I'd rather be poorer and a good father.

Geoff Creelman

Dads should try to find a balance between being too hard and too soft. The only way that can be done is to sacrifice.　　　Geoff Marsh

Cost in time

In terms of time, there is no getting around the fact that you have to give up something. It might be extra time at work, it might be that you decide to put up with the 'danger zone' in the evening at home, it might be that you give up some of your own leisure time, or it might be that you spend less time at conferences.

You may say that this will severely hamper your own life, both personally and professionally. It is worth giving this a little more thought – how would your professional life have been different if, looking back over the past five years, you had made these sacrifices? Would it be markedly different?

Then ask yourself this question: 'If I make the sacrifices, what's the worst thing that could happen to me?' I believe it is highly unlikely that these sorts of decisions would have more than a minor effect, if any, on your professional life. The potential benefits, on the other hand, to your children, yourself and your family, are enormous.

You've got to be honest about it – football is demanding in public and private. But if you decide you always want to be with the kids you can find time. The kids' development has always been at least equal in importance to my sporting career.
                                                            Michael Malthouse

When the kids were young I don't think I spent enough time with them because of my commitments as a journalist and a semi-professional cricketer (I played cricket until I was around 36 years of age). In addition I have spent lots of nights after work and weekends writing books. The book Caught Marsh, Bowled Lillee *was a bestseller, but there are about another 24 books that I've written. I'd finish dinner then I'd go upstairs and spend the evening writing, taping and interviewing people. I feel that I just wasn't there when I should have been. Looking back, a lot of it was self-indulgent, really.*
                                                                Ian Brayshaw

Cost in energy

It's easy to be at home but not focused on the children – the children just run around being children. It takes a certain amount of energy and focus to do the things described in this book, especially if work is tiring, and it's important to understand that.

I am definitely conscious of limiting my work and sacrificing work success in order to spend time with the children. I have chosen to aim at roles in my work that are manageable like that. Probably I'm working within my capabilities rather than on the edge, because working on the edge would have used up my emotional energy and I wouldn't have had enough time for the kids.
                                                            Geoff Creelman

Lots of dads are mentally absent even though they are present in the house. They get so worn down by other people's problems at work that they have no energy left for their life at home, so they are not a lot of fun and they never focus on their kids. Ian Robinson

I wish Dad had been home a bit more and, when he was home, he didn't ignore me and just fall asleep. Mary Kinsella

Cost in dollars

Here I'm not talking about money for books and courses on parenting, but about possible loss of income. I find it very sad to hear businessmen, lawyers and doctors tell me that they hardly get any time with their children, when I know they are earning enormous incomes. When I ask them why they don't go home early, they tell me about what it costs to run their business. If they turn away clients they might lose part of that stream of income. 'So what?' I think to myself.

If they really thought it through, perhaps they wouldn't worry so much. Chasing money is like chasing your tail – it never stops, and you've never finished it – but it really has little to do with fathering. We need to go back and remember what we decided was important in our lives, and make our choices about time and money accordingly.

When my wife Jacqui and I first had children we used to play a silly game, asking how much money would it take for someone to buy our child. A million dollars? A billion? A trillion? The answer was always the same: there was no amount of money that would make up for the loss of a child. And yet all around me I see fathers working hard, making lots of money, but failing to do as good a job of fathering as they want to. If they believed that their failure would cause problems for their children – learning difficulties, the risk of an unhealthy or even dangerous lifestyle, unhappiness or loss of personal integrity and trustworthiness – then surely they would act on it. But no, they keep working late and assuming that their children are going to grow up okay.

There is no way around this fact – being a good dad is going to cost you money. Just for a minute, take the 'price tag' off what you do. What do you do with that money anyway? One day I was driving to the cricket with my ten-year-old son in our Holden Commodore. We were listening to the match on the radio and were hoping to get there in time to see Brian Lara bat. As we were driving there he said to me, 'Dad, how come we don't have a Mercedes like other doctors?' I said that I was in a different branch of medicine and that we couldn't afford it. In any case what would be the difference – we'd still be driving to the cricket, talking to each other and listening to the cricket on the radio and we probably wouldn't notice what car we were in. Worse still, I said, if I had to work enough in my particular type of practice to make enough money to own a Mercedes I wouldn't even have time to go to the cricket with you today. The point is that the economic sacrifice meant that I drove a Commodore instead of a Mercedes but I had time to go to the cricket with my son and talk to him about it along the way.

In the end money is irrelevant. Who cares? The only two things that are really important are having health and having love. Ian Brayshaw

Kylie and I made a decision, because we are both working, that each of us would only work 75 percent of the time. We worked it out so that although we would earn less money we would have more time with the children. One fundamental thing is that any father has to realise that if he wants to spend time with his children, do a good job, it is going to cost him money – he just will not have enough time to earn lots of money. I heard the other day of a business in the eastern states who were interviewing someone for a senior position. At the end of the interview, he asked about the hours and after being told, he said, 'Well, you expect me to work all of those hours and miss out on quality time with my wife and children. That is going to cost you!' and he earned more money. I guess I wished he had made a different decision and chosen to earn less money, but at least he put a value on it. Wayne Cormack

In the end you have to make the choice. I knew that there was a choice between making a million dollars or being a good father. In fact there are lots of choices you have to make like that, not just about money, but sport and other things. Craig Serjeant

If a job comes along that would stop me being able to spend time during the day with my family I just say no.   Patrick Gangemi

Everything I own starts to own me.   Anonymous

Cost in rate of career advancement

Sacrifice could be required in any of the areas that mostly drive people in their career: money, fame, power and meaning. You may have to accept not being as famous, as well known, or as talked about as you would like to be. You may not get that senior position you wanted. You may not be able to change the world and help as many people as you originally wanted to. Fathers who take an involved role in fathering do not miss out on these things in the long term, but in the short term they often do. And, of course, it seems important at the time.

Earlier in this chapter I mentioned a recent study which showed that committed fathers reach the same career levels as anyone else, just more slowly. You need to be patient. Good fathering and ambition are not mutually exclusive.

My advice to young dads is that when the doors start swinging open for you and you have moments of real success and fulfilment in your career, you need to have people around who can step in and tell you to slow down. However, you do need to listen to them – I had people at church say those things but I thought they didn't understand. But they did – I should have listened more. The wisdom of the years says you have to make a choice, a hard choice. Or a series of choices. That's just how it is.   Tim Costello

My observation is that Geoff has forgone lots of career opportunities by choosing to limit his commitment of energy to his work to allow himself to have time and energy for his family. He hasn't gone looking for promotions that could have come his way otherwise, based on his experience and ability. Geoff has also changed his work to accommodate my own work and my own interstate travel with my job as a director of a section in a Commonwealth government department. Geoff tends to do the cooking on the weekend whereas I do it during the week. Geoff also does the shopping, a lot of the washing and helps the kids a lot with their homework and sport. I take the children to music, help with some of the homework, and do most of the other housework and the small amount of

ironing that is really essential – it's amazing how much ironing doesn't really need to be done!
Alice Creelman

While in some work situations it's possible to be a good dad and just as successful, you really have to prepare to make a trade-off. You can't always be 100 percent successful, i.e. reach the highest possible career development point and be a good father. You have to be prepared to sacrifice and make that trade-off. In life you need to generate enough rewards to sustain yourself in all areas – work, family life, community life, etc. Rewards in work alone are never enough to fulfil anyone. Too many corporate men are overly self-centred and unable to pull back on the success curve.
Daniel Petre

Making your workplace 'father-friendly'

Some people think that corporate life is not a place for kids, but I don't think corporate life is in any way different to any other part of life – kids should be welcome.
Warren Reynolds

One good way for men in leadership positions to demonstrate good fathering is to work on creating a father-friendly workplace. Of course all of these ideas apply to working mothers as well.

What you can do as an individual

Here are some practical suggestions for you to consider:

■ **Put photos of the children and their schoolwork up in your office**

The wall above my desk is covered in artwork from the kids. I also have a 'macaroni skeleton' that Amy made at Brownies. The ones that seem to affect people the most are the notes from the kids that say 'I love you, Dad' or the one that Scott wrote when he was about six that says, 'Dad, you are more precious to me than gold.' It's still up there because that sort of note is more precious than gold.

■ **Don't work excessively long hours, and discourage others from doing so**

■ **Be aware that people who are staying late may be avoiding something at home**

It may be family conflict, but it may also be the hard work of parenting at difficult times of the day. Either way, you may be in a position to encourage them to not avoid these problems.

■ **Learn skills at work that could help with your fathering**

I did a course on positive mental attitude at work many years ago and I realised that I ought to incorporate a lot of those practices into my parenting.   Michael Chaney

What you can do as an employer, supervisor, leader

If you are the boss, you can help create a father-friendly workplace in a number of ways.

■ **Support men who make tough decisions to be with their family instead of their work**

Men who make such decisions can be criticised by others who either accuse them of a lack of commitment to work or, more difficult, feel judged themselves because they did not make that same decision for their children and they need a way to justify that.

There have been some recent high-profile examples. Daniel Bradshaw, a Brisbane Lions football player, decided to be with his wife when his son was born rather than play with the team in a final. Tim Fischer, at the time the Leader of the National Party, retired from politics to spend more time with his family. Geoff Marsh quit his job as coach of the Australian cricket team, explaining that being away from his children during long cricket tours was the main reason for his decision.

Generally my own personal experience of work has been pretty much one of 'anti-fathering' and 'anti-family' environments. I was used to CEOs and workaholics who didn't think that family was an important part of life. As an employer I do a number of things with my employees to help them with their family lives. One thing I do is to talk about family commitments with my employees. It's important to be really clear with them that you understand, as their employer, that work is important but that it is second in importance to your family. When I say these things I know it shocks a lot of people. At Microsoft I used to mention it at our monthly work status meeting. I always mention that I expect and understand that family responsibilities and relationships may limit their ability to work.

Daniel Petre

▓ Reward performance, not hours spent at work

Try to reduce the peer pressure to work late and on weekends.

I leave for home very late, but to be perfectly honest I am the first to leave. The peer pressure to be the last to leave for home is enormous.

Michael Lill

I talk with the workaholics about their work practices. One guy said to me the other day 'I worked till two o'clock in the morning' with a sense of pride, expecting to be rewarded for it. I told him that he wouldn't be rewarded for it because that was unacceptable. Either the job was wrong and needed to be changed or he wasn't capable of doing the job he had been given within a reasonable amount of time. Either way something had to change. I measure work output on performance not on time spent. Daniel Petre

▓ Encourage workers to set goals that include personal fulfilment and job satisfaction

Work can really help a father provided it helps him be emotionally fulfilled. If a father does a job that is not emotionally fulfilling then he is likely to come home frustrated because he knows he is not making a difference in life. I get really emotionally fulfilled from my work because it is important work and overall I think it makes me a better parent. Tony Cooke

■ Create a fathers' day/night for kids at work

Encourage fathers to bring their children in to work during the week or during school holidays for lunch or for an afternoon party.

Wednesday nights in the West Australian Parliament are now arranged as a buffet night for families, and it has been terrific to be able to bring in young children. There are kids everywhere and they know they are welcome. Along with a reduction in late night sittings, it has helped improve the family situation. Richard Court

■ Try to schedule meetings at times that do not cut into family time

Peter Costello has younger children than I have. We have arranged to have Cabinet meetings a bit later on Monday mornings so Peter can get a plane up on Monday morning, thus enabling him to spend Sunday evening with his family. John Howard

The second thing I do, and its much harder to do, is to try to create a work environment that allows people to have a family life. For example, I try to cut down unnecessary meetings that take up a lot of time, produce a lot of conversation but don't achieve much. I only call a meeting if it is really necessary, if there is a decision to be made and if all the relevant people are going to be there. When I ran a large development group of 500 people in Seattle I would try not to schedule meetings before nine o'clock or after four o'clock unless there was a crisis. If there is a crisis of course you have to do that but otherwise those times are just not good times for status meetings and project updates. It's important that people realise you can still be productive at work and yet drop your kids at school and get home in time for dinner. Daniel Petre

■ Make children welcome in the workplace. Have special places or activities for them if possible

I like to make kids welcome in the workplace. Whenever I hear the voices of kids at work I like to stop and make a fuss of them. I encourage staff to bring their children into the workplace. Warren Reynolds

When I joined the Trades and Labor Council I worked on ways of making it more family-friendly. Tony Cooke

▪ Be aware that you will be an example, for good or bad, to others, including other children

Overall my career has helped enormously in that I have watched other parents in despair about their children and had to help them think about strategies. Also, I have seen fathers of other children speak and act in ways that were very impressive, and I've tried to emulate them.   Peter Prout

During the week when my father was to be hanged for murder, we had one copper, Bob Woodward, who was doing protective services work with us. I got to know him well and I was envious when he talked about going off with his family in Kings Park. And one of my teachers, Mr Gerry McDonald, in Grade 4 was a good role model. He was a good bloke, decent, caring and with a good sense of humour.   Tony Cooke

▪ Encourage fathers to use their workplace to help teach their own children about work, e.g., its value and its ethics

When the children wanted something I would take them to work in my cleaning business and I would get them to do something, just so they appreciated the value of work. I wanted to teach them that if you don't work you can't get something you want.   Greg Wade

What you can do with your colleagues to improve your workplace's parenting ethos

Ask management to encourage good fathering by:
- making material about families and parenting available to workers;
- allowing time for workers to attend seminars on fathering;
- inviting such speakers to your workplace;
- helping generate creative childcare options;
- being sensitive to family emergencies;
- allowing flexible time for work – starting late, finishing early, having career breaks;
- encouraging job-sharing and part-time work.

I make it clear to staff that they can have time off to do family things if necessary. If they are going to watch one of their kids' soccer match, they don't need to hide behind the 'dental appointment' excuse.   Daniel Petre

Summary

- Trying to be a better dad will benefit your work.

- Develop a more 'human' image in your workplace.

- Gain perspective by getting out of the 'goldfish bowl' of work for a while.

- Become a more relaxed, healthy and interesting person by not overworking and becoming stale.

- Your 'treasure chest' of memories and experiences will be full, so you can relax – it's like knowing you have money in the bank for when you need it.

- You will have a better sex life with your partner.

- The children will become your good friends more and more as they get older, if you are close to them.

- You will have more meaning, love and acceptance in your life.

- You may rediscover how to play and stay on a learning curve.

- Your children may keep you better connected to your community.

- If you don't work out the cost of implementing some of the suggestions in this book, you could fail.

- Show leadership about the importance of fathering.

- Be aware that if anyone is staying late they may be avoiding something at home. You may be able to encourage them to confront these problems.

- Support men who make decisions to be with their family instead of their work.

- Encourage good fathering.

- Make work father-friendly.

 IDEA FOR ACTION:

Schedule one change per week in your work environment to encourage good parenting.

During a Test match series I would often sit in a hotel room in Pakistan, where the food is killing me, just thinking about my kids in their sports on the weekends and realising I would not be there. I used to ring the family as often as possible – until the money ran out or the phone was not able to be connected (in India and Pakistan). After games finished I would rush back to the hotel, desperate to ring home. I asked them about their lives. I have to confess that I usually asked them more about their sports than their homework, but I guess that is just the sort of interest I have.

Geoff Marsh

When I'm overseas I ring every day. Sometimes I only speak for three minutes, but I ask them what they're doing. Often, of course, they're busy, and can't really say much to me, but it's important to ring anyway. I always remember the exams they're doing, their sporting functions and their social events, and I ask them about them.

Peter Le Soeuf

Chapter 7

Work-related travel as a fathering advantage

Snapshot

- Minimising the effects of work-related travel on your children:
  - before you go
  - while you are away
  - when you return

There was this one time I came across my father in the shed just as he was about to head off on one of these extended trips, to relieve at another country police posting. He was crying. He'd stalked off to the shed to have a bit of a weep, you know, so us kids didn't see him and get upset. It was upsetting to see him like that. But it was an important moment for me, to see that he felt it too, that he had no choice but to go. It just made him more human to me. I didn't have to feel abandoned. I knew he'd rather be with us. Maybe this is harder to make clear to a kid when you're a father heading off to Paris or New York. But I try to make it plain to my kids that I'd rather be home with them. And it's true. I don't like being away. I'm a miserable traveller.   Tim Winton

It is common for busy dads to have to travel away from home for long periods. This usually makes fathering hard, and children complain about it. This travel, whether it is to a nearby town, interstate or overseas, is seen as one of the commonest enemies to good fathering. But there are ways to turn it into a positive experience for the children.

If you can't help being away from your family for long periods

In some occupations it is impossible to avoid being away from the family for long periods. If you are a Test cricketer you have to travel overseas to play cricket – it's just part of the job. Similar problems arise for business people with international commitments, scientists with international commitments, tradesmen who have to travel around the state or interstate for their work, and many others. A lot of the ideas presented here are also useful for fathers who live at a distance from their children.

These ideas can help make being away from your children a positive experience, an experience that increases your connectedness to them instead of eroding it. And contrary to what you might expect, it is often less of a problem being away if you have a close relationship with your children and they know that they are loved by you.

If the children have a good relationship with their father then if you are away for a few days of the week it doesn't really matter. They know they are in your thoughts while you are away. John Howard

Test cricketers and federal politicians have some of the worst travel schedules. They can't swoop in and do their business over a few days the way I can. They can be away for months. It is hard for them to be as present to their children as dads like me, who are home most of the time. Yet just as being at home a lot doesn't mean you will be a good dad, similarly, being away a lot doesn't mean you will fail as a dad.

Here are comments from Geoff Marsh and his daughter Melissa about how his job as Australian Test cricket vice-captain, then the national coach, created difficulties.

I am away sometimes between four and eight months of every year. I guess because of my cricket career, it is just 'the price you pay'. It was a nightmare for all the other fathers in the profession too. Now it is different, because people bring their wives – and sometimes their children – with them. It is the same travelling to the eastern states as going overseas – most of the other guys do not have to travel as much, but coming from the west, you still have to travel a lot. You always have to know what is going on with your children so that when you ring them, you can ask them how it went. Geoff Marsh

Dad's travels have never been a problem for us and we have always been 100 percent behind him. Melissa Marsh, daughter of Geoff

And comments from Kim Beazley, Leader of the Federal Opposition, and Hannah, one of his daughters.

Time with my family is the biggest problem I have. Being Leader of the Opposition is the most difficult job I've had with regard to maintaining a family life. One of the biggest problems is lots of weekend work. I am away at least one out of every two weekends. On the whole I deem these arrangements unsatisfactory overall. Kim Beazley

Being an absent dad has by no means made my dad a bad one. It has just meant that Dad thinks he's a bad one, which is ridiculous. There are positives and negatives to any situation, and yes, although it was sometimes painful not having him around all the time, it did mean that you appreciated your time with him much more. There were birthdays that Dad missed, great academic marks that he wasn't the first to hear about – and by the time you were able to tell him they had lost their lustre – and he wasn't able to see your excitement the day you came home with a lead part in your senior play. However, he was there to teach me how to ride a bike, to read me 'The Night Before Christmas' every Christmas Eve (and he still does!), to score me on my diving efforts down at the local pool and to cheer me on during Saturday morning netball. These were important times too, which I appreciate so much more because Dad could experience them first-hand. Hannah Beazley

Here are some travel suggestions for dads to make your travel a positive for your fathering.

Before you go

- Make sure you explain to the children why you have to go.

  This was another recurring theme in the interviews – when a father was away on a work trip but he had told the children why he was going and how important it was, they felt involved and connected rather than resentful. That was easier for politicians and sportspeople, whose activities were reported on the evening news, but also applied to others whose work was low profile. There is a way of making any business trip interesting to children, especially if you describe the possible outcomes of your trip on the people who are involved, including families and children ('if we don't build … those children will miss out on … ').

  By keeping us informed on what he was doing and why, we understood and therefore did not resent his being away … it also made us feel important and helped our self-esteem. Although Dad was away a lot, we never had that perception, partly because we knew it was important. Rebecca Vidler

  We always knew what Dad was doing and he always told us about it, whether it was good or bad. That made us feel involved. He always had the policy of telling us why he was going away and keeping us informed. Mimi Packer

  Although I'm away a lot, the children have always been able to stay a bit connected to me by watching me on TV. They do watch the news when I am on. In fact when Rachel was five years of age she was watching me on the news and she said to her mother, 'There's Kim Beazley, the Prime Minister.' Susie explained to her that no, your father is not the Prime Minister he is the Leader of the Opposition. 'Who is Prime Minister then?' Susie told her it was John Howard. 'Well then why didn't you marry him?' I'm sure she knew what she was saying. She is very sharp. Kim Beazley

- It helps if you tell them how much you will miss them. When they are teenagers they may not give you much of a response, but they will remember, so tell them.

  I suppose the only times I was truly miserable as a child were when one of my parents was away for any period. When Mum had to go to hospital – usually to have a baby. There was a period when I was thirteen or fourteen when my father had to work away for six weeks at a time. He came home on weekends but I just hated it, really hated it. And I knew he did too. It was really traumatic, the times he had to go back. I remember those times most vividly now when I have to go away for work. It's so easy to dismiss the pain of a child separated from a parent. And adults are so good at justifying their own behaviour, minimising kids' emotions. You know, sweeping it under the carpet. Men are great at that.

Tim Winton

I'll never forget those feelings when I flew my Tiger Moth from England to Australia and met up with Jenny at Kalumbaru and then the kids at Broome. The way they greeted me was really special, and I'll never forget it. Each of them said something special like 'Dad you've made it!' or 'Dad, don't go again' or 'Thank goodness you're here.' I really missed them over those six weeks.

Brian Edwards

■ Leave them notes. Hide them in their school bags, under their pillow – wherever. Use the notes to tell them how much you love them or to let them know you know what's going on with them.

I was leaving to catch a plane to Sydney for a flying visit when I realised I had meant to write Scott a note about his exams. Fortunately Jacqui was dropping me at the airport so I quickly scribbled a note:

> Scott. I really admire the way you have worked hard at preparing for these ex ams. I will be thinking of you today in your English test while I am in Sydney and I will be praying for you. I look forward to hearing how it went when I get back tomorrow night. I love you. Dad.

When I was going away to South Africa for two weeks I wrote fourteen letters to Hannah and Lucy before I left. I gave them to Cailey and she fed them out each day, one at a time. Sometimes it was just a picture of where I was going.

Kanishka Raffel

Occasionally I had glimpses that my dad was not totally evil. Before he was hanged he wrote me a note saying he loved me, wishing me all the best for the future. That was very important to me.

Tony Cooke

Not everyone finds it easy to write notes. One reason that this book has been written is to remind you that you don't have to invent it all yourself; you can use ideas from other dads.

The dads I spoke to gave three main reasons for not writing notes to their children.

- **They've just never thought of it.** Having now read this page, that does not apply to you.

- **They're just too busy to write notes to their children.** When I wrote a note recently to my son Scott I timed how long it took. It was 44 seconds. Given that there are 168 hours in every week and if you sleep for 8 hours a night that takes away 56, that still leaves 112. If there are 112 hours in a week, surely you can find 44 seconds to write a note to one of your children every now and again.

- **I just don't know what to say in a note.** Here is a simple suggestion for writing such notes. They could contain three components:

  1 Something about the situation
  'I am thinking of you while you are doing your exams.'
  'I guess you will be reading this during your lunch hour.'
  'You will find this note under your pillow after I have left for my trip.'

  2 Something about them
  'I know you're feeling a bit anxious about that exam.'
  'I know you are very excited about the sports carnival.'
  'I know you've been feeling a bit sad since Grandma died.'

  3 Something about your feelings
  'I just wanted to let you know that I am thinking of you.'
  'I will be missing you while I'm away.'
  'I love you very much and think of you a lot.'
  'I really appreciate the way you handled yourself in that situation.'
  'I know Grandad would be really proud of you for the way you handled yourself.'

'I just wanted to say thank you for the way you've worked hard at getting on with your brother/sister/mother.'

■ Leave stickers such as hearts for each child, on their pillows, schoolbooks, door, bathroom mirror, or any place where you know the right child (not their sister/s or brother/s!) will find the right stickers.

■ Give your children a calendar and a trip itinerary so they know where you are.

■ Before you leave home hide some treasure – a note saying where something is hidden, some lollies, it doesn't much matter what. Draw the treasure map to where you've hidden them, then mail the map home, bit by bit.

While you are away

■ Call them. Phone calls are much cheaper now, and a quick call always helps you stay connected.

In terms of staying in touch, all I can say is thank God for Alexander Graham Bell. I ring Susie about four times a day and Rachel at least once a day. I talk to the older girls more sporadically now, because they have their own lives and it's harder to get hold of them.　Kim Beazley

Being away is my biggest problem – I am away about 25 percent of the time. I try to minimise that and make some positives out of it. I call home at least once a day and often twice a day (the telephone bill for my last overseas trip was exorbitant). I always send my wife flowers when I am away (I will let you into a secret – organise this in advance!).　Glenn Begley

My biggest problem currently is travelling away. I'm away a lot, particularly over the last ten years, since my book was published. When I'm away I always ring every night.　Peter Newman

If I am away Tim feels it more than the girls. We usually talk a lot at home so if I'm not there and the mobile rings first thing in the morning, I know exactly who it's going to be – Tim.　Craig Serjeant

When I am interstate I call at least three to four times each day to ask the kids, 'How has your day been?' Actually, to be perfectly honest, I tend to talk to the kids more when I am away than when I am at home!

Anonymous, businessman

In the last twenty years it's been much easier to phone every day or every other day, and I've done that, but that's because the costs have diminished.
Gus Nossal

What would appear to others to be an unusual upbringing was normal to Dean and myself. Having Dad away for lengthy periods of time for cricket or work is part of our family dynamic and is what we have grown up with. Frequent contact by Dad by telephone maintained an open relationship during these periods and reminded us that he loved us and was thinking of us.
Adam Lillee

- Talk about what is happening in *their* lives (also much easier if you have found out before you go what important things they will be doing while you are away). Know what they are doing – an important sporting event, a school concert, a music concert – and when, so that you can check with them how it went.

Talk about what is happening *to you* (much easier if you have prepared them in advance by telling them why you need to go). Although a mobile phone call from overseas is fairly expensive, a quick call home from interesting spots has a certain magic. I was in Dublin when the World Cup Rugby was on and saw the Wallabies play Ireland. My son is a rugby player so I called him during the game. He wanted to know about the crowd, the game and the number of Aussies there. We still talk about that call.

Sometimes I am away for long periods, for example five weeks at the Atlanta Olympics and four weeks at the Commonwealth Games in Victoria, Canada. When I am away they still see me on TV talking about the results so they stay a bit connected that way. Also I ring about every second night. Sometimes they just say 'hello' and sometimes we talk about school. Often we will talk about what they are watching sport-wise on TV, e.g., 'What about the bomb in Atlanta?' Because I was nearby when the bomb went off I was able to tell them exactly what happened.
Michael Thomson

When they were very young and I was overseas I'd call and talk about having been to the Tower of London or the Eiffel Tower or other things with which they would be familiar. More typically, I'd just ask them about what they were doing.
John Howard

- Email them, and send digital photos if you have access to a digital camera.

  The older girls keep in touch by email. Kim Beazley

  Recently, with email, I've been able to send emails every day, and I have a digital camera, so I send photos of my trip. Peter Le Soeuf

- Write or send postcards.

  Dad sent us all postcards once when he was in Western Australia, telling us how much he loves us. I stuck mine in my locker at school and I still have it. Jessica Anderson

  My father was very busy throughout his 29 years in politics, but he always had time for the family. He travelled extensively, but always wrote to us or phoned us if he was not home. Even today, at 89, he still keeps in touch with his children, grandchildren and great-grandchildren. Richard Court

  Throughout my working life I've averaged about eight to ten weeks away each year. I'm so old-fashioned that I used to write letters home and send handwritten postcards. I didn't keep much contact by phone with the kids because I guess in those days it wasn't the rule to phone – phones were much more expensive than they are now, and there was no email. Gus Nossal

- Send cards with special messages over the Internet. There are many useful websites through which cards can be sent.

- If you are away for a long time, or live a distance away, you can still ring the children's teachers or sports coach and so on to discuss how your child is going. As usual, even if you are unhappy with something the person has said or done, remember that such interactions work better if they begin with:
  'Thanks for your hard work' or 'I really appreciate the fact that you are coaching my son in the football team' or 'Is there anything I can do to help?'

- It helps a lot if your p.artner can at least sound supportive about your trips, about the reasons for them and the fact that you love the children. This is important even if there are underlying feelings of anger, frustration or bitterness.

I ask myself why we did not resent Dad being away all the time. I think it was because Mum was always interested in his work and always supported him in it.
Mimi Packer

- Buy them gifts – this shows you are thinking of them. Of course no amount of gifts will make up for your absence if you don't also make up for it in other ways.

I bring presents home for each child and Sue, on every trip I do. When I get home from every trip, even if I've only been away for two days, they gather around and get their presents.
Peter Le Soeuf

I always bring Merrin and the children gifts, such as books and T-shirts. I always allow half a day for shopping while I am away and any of my postgraduate students who are overseas at the conference with me, I drag along with me. It is part of the ritual of being one of my PhD students.
Glenn Begley

When you come home

- When you come home, don't immediately try to reassert your own rules and ways of doing things. The children have been following other rules while you have been away, and it gets confusing for them if they are expected to change rules immediately. It also undermines your partner.

One of the difficulties I have with travelling is that when I come home from the trip, I start to try to institute my rules on the children; they have had different rules from their mother for the previous few weeks, and that makes it all very confusing. I think it is important that dads who travel a lot do not come in and start rearranging the family rules – it is hard to do that, but it is important.
Glenn Begley

Dad was wise enough to realise that he could not come swanning in and rearrange the family rules – it would be too disruptive and would create uncertainty.
Michael Chaney

- Think about and discuss how you would like to return – do you want a few days to recover? A holiday together? A celebration? Some peace and quiet? In my early days of travelling, the first few days back with the family were tough. I got used to being alone and they were used to my not being there. To make it worse, I used to get extremely badly jetlagged, and would come home grumpy. My wife suggested, tongue-in-cheek, that I go to a motel for my first two days back from any long trip. I have learnt to handle this better now, and I make my travel less hectic.

- Make it up to them when you get home, in time and attention.

When I came back from my travels, I would always make sure that I spent all my time with them. They always knew that I would be totally focused on the family when I got home. One of the secrets of that is to live within your means. You cannot do that sort of thing if you have overspent and, when you return from your travels, you do not have the time to spend with your children because you have to work really hard to continue to pay off your mortgage. Geoff Marsh

The kids were never miserable because Geoff was away – he used to ring them all the time, and when he came home it was always quality time with the children. They did not plan anything else – the kids knew they were top priority. Michelle Marsh

Other things to be aware of

- If you start a new job that requires a lot of travel, and your previous jobs didn't, your being away will have a greater effect on the children than if all your jobs have involved lots of travel.

My being away was easier for my children because they grew up with me not being there much. Shaun would have been just two years old when I started travelling. Geoff Marsh

- If you know that extensive travel away from home will be part of your job, make strategic decisions with your partner about her work and your own work, whether you will need to live close to supportive family members and so on. If she can't get the support she wants then you should ask whether the job is worth it.

We were helped by having grandparents around a lot, so the kids have a strong extended family. If the father is going to be away a lot, it is a good idea to make a decision to live near at least one set of grandparents so that the children have extended family to support them – the kids can spend some time with their grandparents. My father Ross often took the kids to their sport.

Michelle Marsh

- Avoid too much travel when your children are young – they need you more then, and are too young to understand why you are going. For instance, because I had formed such a strong bond with my son, whenever I had to go away to a conference, he got very upset. Once I had to fly off to Miami for four days for a conference, and we decided not to tell him I was going. On the day of my departure, he noticed the suitcase and came running into the kitchen area with tears streaming down his cheeks. We tried to console him but it was very difficult. We decided that it was not a good idea just to sneak out; it was better to explain carefully to him the reasons why I had to go.

I decided not to travel as much to medical conferences when the children were younger. I travel a lot more now that they are more independent, but I felt that when they were younger I needed to be at home more.

Ian Frazer

Avoid being away on their birthdays if you possibly can. I recall once agreeing to give a lecture at a symposium in Rotterdam a few days after attending a major meeting in the USA. What I had not realised was that by the time I spoke at the meeting in Rotterdam and got a return flight and flew home, I would have missed my son's sixteenth birthday. I had a difficult decision, but in the end, I cancelled the Rotterdam trip. I found someone else suitable to speak but it caused them some inconvenience. I know I let them down and I should have planned this in advance so as to not inconvenience them, and I apologised to them, but I just could not miss my son's sixteenth birthday. Now, as I look back, I am glad I made that decision, as much for my sake as for his – he may not remember that I was there but he might have remembered if I wasn't. Anyway, I would remember.

I haven't missed many birthdays, especially when they were young, except perhaps when parliament was sitting. It's all part of making them feel that they're very important.
John Howard

If one of you is away a lot, it may be difficult for the other one to work full-time. This is a tough issue, but no tougher than other similar issues in a relationship where one person is away or very busy a lot of the time.

I did not work when Geoff was playing Test cricket because I realised that one of us had to fill the gap. I am working now, though.   Michelle Marsh

Summary

Before you go

- Make sure you explain to the children why you have to go.

- It helps if you make sure they know how much you will miss them. When they are teenagers they won't give much of a response, but they will remember, so tell them.

- Leave notes for them – hidden in their school bags, under their pillow – telling them how much you love them or letting them know you know what's going on in their lives.

- Leave stickers on their pillows, schoolbooks, doors, the bathroom mirror ...

- Give your children a calendar and a trip itinerary so they know where you are.

- If you are going for a long time, put a photo of yourself and some notes on their pillow and (if possible) make a video they can play when you are away.

- Hide some treasure for them. Draw a treasure map, then mail the map home, bit by bit.

While you are away

- Keep in touch: call them, email them (and send digital photos if you have access to a digital camera), send cards with special messages over the Internet, write or send postcards.

- Know what they are doing – an important sporting event, a school concert, a music concert – and when, so you can check with them how it went.

- If you are away for a long time, or live a distance away, you can still ring the children's teachers, sports coach, and so on to discuss how your children are going.

- Partners need to be at least verbally supportive of your trips, of the reasons for them, and of the fact that you love your children.

Coming home

- When you come home, don't immediately try to reassert your own rules and ways of doing things.

- Think about and discuss how you would like to return – do you want a few days to recover? A holiday together? A celebration? Some peace and quiet?

- Make it up to them when you get home, in time and attention.

- Buy them gifts – this shows you are thinking of them. Of course no amount of gifts will make up for your absence if you don't make up for it in other ways as well.

General tips

- If you start a new job that requires a lot of travel, and your previous jobs didn't, your being away will have a greater effect on the children than if all your jobs have involved lots of travel.

- Make strategic decisions with your partner – about your partner's work, whether you will need to live close to supportive family members and so on – if you know that extensive travel away from home will be part of your job.

- Avoid too much travel when they are young; they need you more then and are too young to understand why you are going.

- Avoid being away on their birthdays if possible.

 IDEA FOR ACTION:

Before your next work trip, plan to tell your children about its importance and what you will be doing while you are away.

I love the way Dad gives each of us a shot to spend about a month with him so we can talk by ourselves and have practically 100 percent of the time with him, except for some meetings he has to go to. We went to Sydney, Los Angeles, San Francisco, Calgary, Chicago, Pittsburgh, England and Paris. On the trip I did a journal and one

question was how does Dad feel. He said 'I love being with my daughter'.   Amy Robinson

Although the overseas trips were associated with Dad's work, that never got in the way. Overall the feeling was a very positive one of having an adventure together.   Jane Perkins

Chapter 8

Take kids on work trips

Snapshot

- When to take the children with you
- What to do with them
- Work trips as educational adventures

The idea of taking kids with you on work trips was one of the most powerful suggestions made by the interviewees, and it was supported by the comments of their children. It is another way to make your work a friend of your fathering. The experiences described by these children make me think that every dad who has to be away from home for work should do this.

These are the key aspects:

- Take one child at a time.
- No other adults should come.
- It doesn't have to be overseas or interstate – the next town will do.
- Stay overnight, if possible.
- Make time to do some non-work things together.
- Plan the trip with your child.

Local work trips are easy, cheap and valuable

Local trips, such as going bush with the children, are easy to do. Kids love sitting in the car talking to Dad. The idea of having Dad alone for a while so you can talk to him is very attractive.

When I wanted to talk to Dad as a teenager, I would invite myself on one of his long trips. That way I could sit in the car with him and have him to myself for a couple of hours.
Jane Perkins

It doesn't have to cost a lot to have special times with the children.

You don't have to go to Paris to do this stuff. My dad used to take me with him on slow days in the paddywagon. We'd pull over on some quiet country road and shoot rabbits for a while and then he'd deliver a summons or something. I've taken the kids on trips to country towns, done a job on the Friday and made a weekend of it, a bit of an adventure, a few larks.
Tim Winton

Kids aren't looking for the big things like overseas trips and things like that, they need attention and time – that's all they ask for. Just take them out, for example go fishing or eat out.

Eric Tang

If you are doing a job in the country for a few days or weeks, think about taking one of the children along with you.

My dad was a builder in the country and often he would take us with him. We would stay in various places like caravans and help him a bit e.g., painting, sweeping and shovelling. He'd pay us a bit. Also on those trips we'd go fishing or something else after a few days. We still talk about those times and laugh. The blokes who worked with him were real characters. They all seemed to be very happy in what they were doing and always cracking jokes, even if it was over 100° Fahrenheit every day. That taught me that you can have fun in your work and that you shouldn't take your work too seriously. I like the phrase 'You work for a living, you don't live to work.' Michael Thomson

Sometimes we would drive up north in the station wagon, sleeping in the back along the way. They were great adventures. Once we drove along a rough track into Pannawonica, and when it got dark we had to stop. I got freezing cold and all we had was a sheet of black plastic, which we fought over all night. Jock Clough

Take them to conferences

When I first started going to work conferences it was rare to find children there with their parents. Now it is reasonably common – some of the major conferences provide childcare facilities now, so that there are interesting things for children to do while their parents are working.

I don't believe my work suffered a lot on trips when I took the kids. Of course as a driven person, my preference was to do everything, go to everything, maximise my trip, but even when I didn't achieve this, I really didn't miss much that mattered in the long run. I became much more selective, and attended only those conferences, clinics and laboratories that were of most relevance on each trip. Good planning is important for this.

My first work trip with my oldest son

Taking my kids with me on work trips has been one of the best experiences of my life. When my oldest son, Simon, was around eight years old, I decided that I would take him with me on a conference trip. About six months before the trip, I was sitting at Heathrow Airport, near London. I thought about my decision and groaned – I was jetlagged, the plane was late and I was sure that having to worry about a nine-year-old child as well as myself was going to make it all extremely difficult. How wrong I was.

This trip lasted about a month. My son was nine at the time. He visited his grandparents and other relatives in England, saw friends in Boston and Washington DC, went to Disneyland and visited other relatives in Sydney. Along the way I worked hard, attending conferences, hospitals and research laboratories. In towns where I had friends or relatives, they looked after my son while I worked.

It is eleven years ago now but I remember my month-long overseas trip with Dad very well. It felt good because I thought 'there's Dad doing his important conference stuff and here's me going as his mate'. It was different to going with the whole family – this was just with Dad. It was the first big thing we ever did alone together. Other things like camping we had done with other family members, usually all of us. It was special and good fun just being with Dad. I felt like I was on a conference trip as well. Simon Robinson

It is impossible for me to express how much I enjoyed that trip. I enjoyed sitting in airports with my son, sitting next to him on the plane, sitting waiting for trains at railway stations, hiring a car and just travelling with him. When we returned home and he went back to school, I missed his company a lot.

It was very special travelling overseas with Dad on conference trips. We had a great time together going to Singapore and Amsterdam.

Jonathan Begley

Work trips with the other two kids

When my second son, Scott, reached the age of ten we did a similar trip. Although all the children have had some common destinations (they all wanted to visit Disneyland), they each had an otherwise different itinerary.

On my overseas trip with Dad we went to the footy in Melbourne and saw Collingwood beat the Eagles by 36 points and Brett Spinks nearly broke his neck going for a hang. We went to Disneyland and Universal studios. In San Diego, I loved the zoo, Baltimore Bagels and Ben and Jerry's Apple crumble ice cream. We saw a car and motorbike crash right in front of us near where we stayed with Courts and Damien. We stayed in a log cabin in the Rocky Mountains and drove around in a rented silver T-bird full of gadgets. In England we saw family.

I enjoyed spending time with my dad, like being next to each other on plane trips. You talk to other kids at school and the majority have never been anywhere or done anything special with their dads. They ask me what I've done and I tell them and they say 'gee, you're lucky'. It makes me think 'wow'. But it's not like their dads don't love them. It's just that Dad makes an effort and that makes me feel special, that I really mean something to him. Scott Robinson

My daughter Amy's trip was similar: we visited friends in Canada, went snowboarding in the Canadian Rockies and, at the end of our trip, had a weekend in Paris. I confess that on the last night before we were due to fly back, tears came to my eyes – I had enjoyed these trips so much, and I realised that this was the last one I would be doing with my children in that way. Of course there would be other trips, but not these special one-month trips at that age.

Others have also found this sort of trip to be a great experience with their children.

The toughest part has been the travel. I don't do much any more, but for a couple of years it was like a treadmill. So Denise and I figured out ways I could include the kids in the trips. I'd cut my cloth to fit, so to speak, do the lightest possible workload and travel with company. Each of the kids came on a trip with me to London or Paris. Like a rite of passage. Maybe for me more than them! But it was great. Each of them had this thing about the Nôtre Dame cathedral. They read the Hugo novel about the Hunchback and they'd seen the Charles Laughton movie (this was before the Disney crap), so they wanted to see this cathedral. It was fun going to cities I knew well and seeing them in a different way, from a different height, if you like, with a child. It's quite a challenge to travel alone with a child, but such a blast. They were special times. Two weeks in the same room, the same bed most of the time. Throw in a foreign language and a few long flights – bingo! I've done shorter trips in Australia with them, too. You'd be surprised what you can get done, even with a seven-year-old, if you're flexible and you don't have silly expectations. I remember those trips vividly. The ones I did alone are a bit more of a blur by comparison. I think the kids learnt a lot from those trips. About language and culture and architecture, how other people do things. They each kept journals and scrapbooks. It helped our relationship and it helped my work. You tell a lot of stories to a kid in trains and on planes and in hotel rooms. The presence of a child changes the tenor of a business meeting. You learn a bit about yourself. And I wrote a novel, The Riders, *about a bloke travelling with his daughter. Couldn't have done it otherwise.*   Tim Winton

Because my job entails a lot of travel, I've also been able to take the family with me. We've done lots of trips together. My most memorable one is probably when we went around Europe visiting 40 cities in six months. I was on study leave, and my job was to study the transport patterns in those cities.   Peter Newman

I have not actually taken the children individually on work trips. I regret that. I have endeavoured to put the family first, but the pressures of work sometimes prevented me from doing that. Michael Chaney

At what age?

The answer to this depends on the type of trip. For overseas trips, the general consensus among those interviewed is that any age between about seven and ten is good: the children are old enough to be easily managed, they know how to use a mobile phone, they know what to do if they get lost, and so on. They are also old enough to prepare for the trip, to keep a journal, and to remember what you did together.

Take them one at a time

Travelling with other adults means the adults talk together, and taking more than one child at a time means they talk with each other. So take the children one at a time.

I travel a lot with my work, but I've tried to use my travel to take the kids with me. I've taken Tim on three trips, one to Austria and Switzerland, one to Seattle, Chicago and the Indianapolis 500, and another one to South America. I did a trip with Anna to Canada, Bermuda, England and Washington DC, and a trip with Kate to London, Buenos Aires and Venezuela, with a side trip to Angel Falls. I usually use frequent flyer points when I take the kids. Peter Le Souef

What to do with the kids while you work

At some conferences I used the conference childcare service. Sometimes partners of colleagues who were attending the conference took my children shopping with them.

Where my work was close to a hotel, I would try to book a room there, so my child could easily walk from his/her room to where I was. I also walked it through with them, showing them exactly where I would be if they needed me (on those occasions they often preferred to watch TV in the hotel room, though).

Occasionally they sat in on my work sessions. Sometimes I gave them a Gameboy or something to occupy them – that only works for a while. Give them a mobile phone so they can call you, wherever you are.

On these trips, your child may take about 50 percent of your attention – that is 50 percent of your scheduling time, 50 percent of your time and up to 50 percent of your budget. In my experience, the investment is worth many times that.

Talk to the children in advance about what your expectations are and what their expectations are.

Somehow, I forget exactly how, I came by the idea of taking my eldest boy (Matthew), who was eight years old at the time, to a meeting in Sydney in 1991. We struck a deal – he would come along with me to most of the major scientific presentations and, in exchange, I would take him to one or two more 'touristy' highlights of Sydney. He chose a visit to Taronga Zoo and a ferry ride to Manly. We also ate out at night with other scientists at the conference. Michael Good

Prepare for the trip by creating expectations that add to the enjoyment.

I have a photo of Harry standing in front of Nôtre Dame when he was eight or so. It stops me in my tracks some days, the smile on his face. He's the one passionate about art. He wanted to see Van Goghs and he wanted most of all to be inside the cathedral of Nôtre Dame. In the photo he's been in Paris about fifteen minutes and he's standing out on the parvis in front of the cathedral with the biggest grin. I remember him spouting on about Gothic this and that in the freezing wind and both of us laughing and excited that he'd finally made it. Now when I see the photo I have this image of a kid I've managed to make happy. I hardly recall the professional things I did that trip, but I remember what we did together. Tim Winton

The reason I am so happy in this picture is because I waited my whole life to be there. Dad and I had a great time together and it is a moment that I'll remember all my life.   Harry Winton

Taking them out of school

I have always tried to overlap these trips with their vacation time but, as the trips last three to four weeks, they do miss out on some school time. Some parents are very nervous about this. I would encourage you not to be. Here are some of the reasons why:

I used to take them up to the north of the state when I was treating Aborigines in the North-west. This was a very rich time for them because they saw lots of the bush and even went to corroborees. Often they were the only white kid amongst lots of black kids. We drove around in jeeps. I didn't mind taking them out of school for these things.   Ian Constable

The timing of the meeting also meant that Matthew did not miss out on school. However, even if the conference did not occur during school holidays it would be easy to make the argument that the child's education benefited by visiting Sydney for a few days.   Michael Good

Reason 1 – Knowledge of a different sort

My children learnt a huge amount of stuff that was educationally useful on their trips with me, even though what they learnt was not on their current school curriculum and thus not 'examinable'. In fact I am sure they learnt more efficiently than if they had stayed at school for those extra days.

Each child filled out a journal, the model of which was kindly prepared by one of their teachers, Dorothy Tribe. She did one for each of the children from then on, even if she wasn't their teacher at the time. It included spaces for recording trip details, aircraft information, currency, weather, interesting people, new languages, new foods and special experiences, along with space to glue in various bits of memorabilia. These journals remain treasured possessions, and the children still pull them out and look at them from time to time.

Reason 2 – You can include educational concepts

You can use the one-on-one time to teach them whatever they would have been learning in class had they been at home. Fortunately, their teachers were aware of that too. They didn't give me a detailed program of study for the children, because they knew we would be struggling to follow it, but they told me in general terms what the kids would have been studying and asked me to incorporate those things into the trip.

With Simon, for example, it was time to learn fractions. When he and I were sitting on a railway station somewhere in rural England, waiting for a train, I bought a chocolate bar and proceeded to break it up into pieces, teaching him what fractions of the whole piece the bits were as I went. We spent about 30 minutes doing that and he learnt his fractions easily that way.

Reason 3 – Valuable learning experience

Children go to school for about twelve years. That is about 2400 days. Does it matter if you take them out for 10 days? That still leaves 2390 days. Taking a few days off school to go away with their father is guaranteed to be a good learning experience – it can only have a positive impact on their learning overall.

Reason 4 – Getting close to your children

When a child's school performance suddenly starts to decline, there is usually an identifiable reason, and that reason is most commonly related to how the child feels about life. Children who feel loved, secure, valued and accepted are in the best emotional state to learn well. It would be hard to think of a more powerful way to tell a child these things than being prepared to spend a few days or weeks alone with them, making them a priority, doing things that they want to do, talking with them and having fun with them.

Impact on the kids

How could a child not think such trips are special? When my second son was finishing primary school, each of the students in his year was interviewed and asked about the highlights of their time in primary school. I was videoing my son's interview and heard him say that one of his highlights was travelling round the world with his father the year before. I wasn't expecting him to say that and I felt a tear trickle down my cheek as I was videoing. One always assumes that these types of trips make an impact on the kids, but it was nice to hear it from him.

I have asked a dozen or so children who have done these sorts of trips with their dads what they think about them in retrospect and, not surprisingly, they all loved them.

His mother observed that Matthew enjoyed the trip enormously and he appreciated greatly the opportunity to spend some dedicated time with his father.
Michael Good

As an only child with a single parent I received a great deal of undivided attention, and by and large that was a very positive experience. With a large family of my own now (Paula and I have eight children) it is uncommon for my children to receive such undivided attention. So I take my kids to conferences with me. To date six of my children have now accompanied me to conferences, with the two older children both having been to two conferences. By about the age of sixteen they appear to be less interested in accompanying their Dad to conferences – not 'cool' – but I believe they will hold their time spent with me at the conferences in a special way.
Michael Good

When I am at home it is hard to find time for each of the children as individuals, so what I have done is take each of them off to conferences at various times. My sons have been interstate, to other Australian cities or overseas – for example, to the USA, Singapore and Amsterdam. These trips are very special to the children.
Glenn Begley

What to do when you're not working

Be a bit adventurous – do something neither of you has done before.

Family trips overseas, particularly if they're a bit adventurous, are very special for a family because of the element of taking risks, a bit of the going-into-the-wilderness type feeling. It generates a bit of insecurity and that adds to the feeling of it being worthwhile. Standard life is secure and easy, which is important to enable the kids to function normally, but special times with a bit of adventure are important and different.

Peter Newman

I am taking the two oldest boys to Fraser Island (in Queensland) in October while I attend a conference. We plan to have some time whale-watching together and doing other things. We have done some big family trips – a ski trip to the USA and Disneyland and ten days in Canada together.

Paul Bannan

Some of the most wonderful bonding experiences I've had with my children were a couple of weeks with each of them on different overseas trips, just with one of the children, particularly in difficult and adventurous circumstances. These have made us really close. Peter Le Soeuf

My job has created opportunities for me to have special times with the children, such as when they come over to Canberra, and when they come on special trips. For example last year Rachel came with me to visit five Aboriginal communities. I thought it would be a good way for her to understand Aboriginal communities. She was fascinated by the Aboriginal kids and by free camping. Kim Beazley

Take them to major events, be they sporting, musical or wherever *their* interests lie.

Because I have to commentate on a lot of sporting events during school holidays, we've tried to overcome the problem by bringing the family over to those events. For example we would often have Christmas in Melbourne around the Boxing Day Test and then we would travel together to Sydney and Brisbane. We would stay in the best hotels. These holidays have created some special memories for the children. They speak fondly of these times. Also, I'd take the family overseas with me on trips, for example to the end-of-season football matches. Dennis Cometti

Where to stay

I have used a mixture of approaches on my trips with the children. I have found that staying with friends is a good way to manage the combination of work and travel. Your child will meet 'the locals' and your friends can help you look after your child while you work.

Hotels are also fun, especially as they don't dilute the one-on-one experience. I have used youth hotels/ backpacker accommodation too, with the specific aim of helping the children feel comfortable with that style of travel – it may be useful if they want to explore the world when they are older.

We stayed, inexpensively, at one of the residential colleges at Sydney University. This was possible because this conference is held in December, when university college students have gone home for holidays. The rules were simple: the child had to be eight years old, they had to spend a great deal of time at the conference, I would take them to two or three highlights of the city, and we would stay at university colleges, which are not only inexpensive but also handy to the conference site, which is usually on campus.
Michael Good

'Will workmates disapprove if I bring one of my kids along?'

I have never heard anyone complain about my bringing my children. Even when they are in the conference hall with me and I am chairing and speaking in front of hundreds of people I have never heard complaints. Quite the contrary – colleagues like to meet my children and they like the whole idea of bringing them along. It has stimulated them to do the same.

In the nine years that I have been taking my children to this conference, never once has a scientist at any of the conferences complained to me that my children should not have been there. In fact, the reverse is true – a number of people have told me that they enjoyed the children's presence at these conferences.
Michael Good

'How often can I do this?'

The frequency of such trips depends, of course, on the nature of your work, the expense involved and the type of trip you are doing. Local trips to country towns are easier to pull off than complicated overseas trips, and are more manageable economically.

My approach has been to do one big trip lasting about a month when they are each around ten years old, with smaller trips – for four to seven days, for example – after that when it is convenient. Others tend to do lots of smaller trips. Some friends take their children on a trip pretty much each year.

At least once each year we have done a trip that has been associated with work.
Anonymous, salesman

Taking the family for long periods

A number of professions provide opportunities for interstate or overseas work, study leave, sabbatical leave, and so on. It is usually economically difficult to make these trips – they can cost! – and they can seem, at first glance, to be disruptive to the children's education and other regular activities. Despite all this, I was amazed at how often the men and women interviewed who had undertaken such trips described these experiences as being some of the richest of their life, certainly things that they would not trade for any amount of money. The children seem to have benefited enormously from the experience, and not to have suffered at all educationally.

Use any opportunity you get to take family on long study leave/work trips, even though it is complicated with the kids' schooling – the family adventure far outweighs the hassle and cost.

The best period I had for having time with the kids was when I was a postgraduate student overseas. I had lots of time with the family then. When Allison was pregnant with Rebecca she needed to have a rest in the afternoon so Liz and I would go off exploring Durham in her pusher. We would chat away to each other for the whole of that time. It was very special. Allan Chapple

Another great time together was a year of sabbatical in Oxford. In fact, you know, I think the kids hardly went to school. We just spent lots of time together as a family. Peter Le Soeuf

I went overseas and did research for five years in Boston. Research is a bit like extended student life. We didn't have much money and didn't know anyone, so we spent most of our time together. I used to take the kids into work on weekends when they were young and we went on camping trips and other holidays together. We fished and did things like picking apples. We never went to the movies because we couldn't afford it. In fact, I only did two things at that time: I worked and I played with the children.

Ian Constable

Also, I have been able to take the whole family to Cambridge (England) on sabbatical for six months, which was a wonderful time together.

Ian Frazer

If you don't do work-related trips, contrive one

A couple of the fathers interviewed told me they actually contrived work-related trips so that they could spend time with their children!

Summary

■ Take one child at a time, and no other adults should come.

■ The best time to start taking your child overseas is when they are between seven and ten.

■ It doesn't have to be overseas or interstate – the next town will do.

■ Stay overnight if possible.

■ Workmates rarely complain if you bring your children along.

■ Plan the trip with your child.

■ Work out your expectations and theirs in advance.

■ Don't worry about taking them out of school: these trips are useful educationally.

■ The trip will have a positive impact on their learning overall.

■ During your work trip, do some non-work things together.

■ Take your child to the conference.

■ Stay with friends along the way – it's a good way to combine work and fun.

■ Make and maintain the memories – make a video, take photos, keep a journal.

 IDEA FOR ACTION:

Plan where and how you might take each of your children with you – just you – on a trip when they are old enough.

My dad was my best role model. We were very close and we had a lot in common, particularly football. Dad and I would go to the football when I was a kid and, when I was playing football, he was there for me every week. Dad was never pushy and didn't want any of the reflected glory or anything. When I was a league coach I noticed lots of dads having a second go through their sons. Dad wasn't like that.

Dennis Cometti

I value the extended family we have. It's a great environment for me. Sometimes the input I get from the family is helpful, but not always. I find it an important source of information but you need to be discerning, and don't just take it all on board without thinking about it. If I think it is true I embrace it, but if I don't I leave it alone.

Patrick Gangemi

Chapter 9

The challenges of being a dad today

Snapshot

- The importance of good fathering
- How changes to work, family structure and community values affect fathering today

What is a good dad?

There are good dads, but they are not always obvious. There are bad dads too, and they are also not always obvious. What is the difference? What does being a 'good dad' really mean?

There are a lot of misleading ideas about 'good dads' and 'bad dads'. The notion that a good dad always comes home from work early, and that men who stay at work late are all bad dads, is ridiculous. There are plenty of dads who come home early and never engage with their children, never think about what their children need from them, and never show love and acceptance of, or belief in their children. And you don't have to look very far to find dads who work long hours and have wonderful relationships with their children. The rules of the game are not as simple as that.

CONSIDER THIS

How do you rate yourself as a dad?

Poor   Average   OK   Pretty good   Excellent

I try to do a good job as a dad because I have always felt that if I failed as a parent it would devastate me.

Craig Serjeant

Bad dads

I would like to be able to say that bad dads are rare and obvious. We all do our best, usually with almost no training and often with poor role models. But there are dads who have not done a good job of fathering.

My father was a terrible role model. He was 99 percent dickhead.

Anonymous, businessman

I was always afraid of my father. Whenever I was in his presence I was scared and tense. He always abused me and put me down and told me I was useless.

Anonymous, farmer

Recently I watched The Australian Story *about Tony Cooke, whose father was the serial murderer in Perth and was hanged when Tony was still in primary school. It was amazing to hear about all the things he* [Tony] *had to put up with at school, and yet he has turned into such a wonderful person and is highly successful. He recently sat in front of me at a conference I was at and I wrote him a note, saying how much I admired him and what he had achieved and I handed it to him. He just turned around at me and smiled and said, 'Thanks, Ken. I really appreciate that.'*

Ken McAullay

I do not have a lot of good role models. My father was not much of a role model. I had a complete lack of a father figure. He was an alcoholic, and when friends came around to visit he was often drunk and embarrassing, so I tried not to bring them around.

Anonymous, athlete

My father was a negative role model, mostly because of his boozing. Also, he was emotionally distant – mostly we never knew how he felt unless he was in a bad mood. Dad was either busy somewhere else or was home and grumpy. He was basically either absent or drunk. His drinking meant that he lost all authority. He was someone to be tolerated but not emulated.

Anonymous, pastor

A lot of my fathering has been done in reaction to the way I was fathered. Of course I have been away a lot, but I would like my kids to forgive me for that and my other mistakes. I know I don't forgive my father, but then the difference between my dad and me is that I really love my kids and I tell them. He told me I was useless, but I've been successful in business and most other things I have tried in life. I wish my dad could see me now.

Anonymous, businessman

One reason that I have worked hard at being a good father is that my own father was such a poor role model.

Peter Prout

I've learnt about how to be a father by trying to be the antithesis of my dad. He was an absent, uninterested father so I try to be present, interested and engaged with my kids.

Anonymous, computer programmer

A bad dad is someone who is uninterested in his children, distant and unloving, unaccepting of children as people and/or who is emotionally or physically abusive. These behaviours eat at the heart of kids' basic needs, which are discussed in detail in Chapter 1.

There are great dads

My dad was a great role model. I was very close to him. He was a plumber and I wanted to be an apprentice to him. He would have just loved to see me as an apprentice.   Seamus Doherty

My parents were great role models because they put their two sons way before their own interests at all time.

Craig Serjeant

I had no idea at all about fathering when I started. I guess I followed the example of my father. He was a pretty good dad. He was detached, but only in so much as it was characteristic of his era. It wasn't really a characteristic of him. He wasn't authoritarian, had lots of wisdom and was kind and calm. He was reliable and always there. He was patient and modest. I guess he has been the biggest influence on how I do my fathering.   Peter Le Soeuf

A good dad is not someone who simply provides for his children and disciplines them; he is someone who meets their needs.

There is no ideal, model father

There can be no 'ideal, model father' – everyone is different, so being a 'good dad' actually means something different for everyone. After reading this book, perhaps you will be able to work out what it means for you.

THE CHALLENGES OF BEING A DAD TODAY

Your style of fathering will depend upon whether you are an extrovert or an introvert, whether you are married or not, whether your partner is in paid employment or not, your economic circumstances, your working hours, any specific problems you or any of your children have in areas of education, health, emotional state and beliefs/values, your own life experiences, and a million other things.

In general, I think men and women are basically equivalent in what they can give children, but we are all different, and it all depends on what our individual personalities are like.

Michael Chaney

There is no one right way to father. There is no one way to go, one thing to do, one place to live, one way to live. There are lots and lots of ways and they are all likely to be valid for your family. Tim Willoughby

Also, every child is different, and good fathering means that we need to understand the personalities and life experiences of each of our children. This will let us work out what their needs are and what is the best way to respond to them.

It's really important to understand each kid's personality and respond accordingly rather than having one general response for all the kids.

Kanishka Raffel

Being a good dad is not just about time, although work hours can be a problem. There are plenty of hours in the week to do the right thing as a father, plenty of ways to be flexible with work time and plenty of ways in which the time you spend at work can help your fathering. Failing as a dad has more to do with whether we know and respond to the things our kids really need from us than with our work schedules.

Good fathering is also essential for fathers

Why is it that when I have to tell middle-aged men that they have cancer and they are going to die (something I have to do often), they mostly tell me that they regret not having spent more time with their children? In saying this they are often not thinking about how the kids have turned out – they are thinking about themselves, and the joys and pleasures that warm, loving family life provides. They realise that the deepest joys and the richest experiences are shared times with those we love. These patients then change their lifestyle and, in their remaining months, start doing things with their children, and saying important things to them. They come back and tell me about it, saying 'I wish someone had told me to do this years ago.'

Hearing that so often over my 26 years in medicine has made me a little frustrated with my fellow dads. Of course most men don't get cancer while their children are young, but some still struggle to have good relationships with their kids and can end up with distant, even bitter relationships which are hard to heal.

Chairman of McDonalds Australia, Peter Richie, honestly reported recently that his relationship with his only son has broken down, and that he blames the fact that he devoted long hours to building up the fast food chain in Australia for that. He is trying to repair the relationship, but it is hard.

The message is that you just can't ignore your family while pursuing a career. My relationship with my son still suffers. He is paying the price for my neglect. As I discovered, you can't catch up for lost time. In the end it's just not worth it.   Peter Richie

He is not the only one to realise this.

I knew an old man who became bitter in his late life. He was consumed by angry regret over his estrangement from his children. He had allowed the demands of his job to come between him and them and by the time he realised what was happening, they had lost interest in him. Even more tragically, he was angry with himself for having lived what he had come to regard as a life made meaningless by its emphasis on short-term gratification, although everyone else had considered him successful. His pain was intensified by the realisation that it was all too late. He was powerless to change anything. Hugh Mackay

Having no dad or a bad dad doesn't mean you will be one too – you have a choice.

Being aware of the real needs of children and understanding what good fathering really is can make men question whether their own dads did a good job or not. It is important to understand the differences between generations and not judge our own fathers as we would judge ourselves. But then there are some dads who really were poor fathers. Does that mean that their sons will be programmed the same way? Most definitely not.

It was clear from the interviews that men who had no dad or whose dad was a terrible role model, even abusive, could become great dads themselves. Sometimes this could be related to alternative male role models and sometimes to the quality of the mothering they received but in the end they all realised something: they had a choice in the matter. They could choose to father the way they were fathered or they could choose a different path.

That was one of the most encouraging things to come out of these interviews and, I guess, represents a major underlying theme of this book – you can choose how you do your fathering, and the choices you make will make a big difference to your children.

As a father, don't expect to be the same as your father. In fact that's an active choice you have to make – choose not to expect to be like your father. If your father was a fantastic father you don't have to expect to be as good as him. If your father was terrible you don't have to assume that you are going to be terrible. Men whose fathers were physically abusive often feel really guilty if they smack the kids and say, 'It's just the way I am – I guess I'm just like my dad after all'. Men can choose to be different and they should.   Tony Cooke

When I was 21, I was into everything that wasn't good for you, but then I got married and had a daughter. Because I had no father I decided I wanted to give my daughter something that I never had for myself – a good father. I had no strong father role models myself so I learnt by reading the Bible to find out what was required of me. I learnt about what a loving father is by learning about God's character, particularly his unconditional love for me. I also learnt a bit by watching other dads in the church. I always felt that eventually I wanted to die knowing that I had done my best as a dad.   Harley Hayward

I hope reading this book helps you with your fathering, so that you do not end up saying, when it is too late, 'I wish someone had told me to do this years ago.'

Why is it hard being a dad today?

While it might seem that fathering should be easier today, because of our high standards of living, the availability of transport and technology etc, it is not. The main reasons for this are:

- changes in the way we work;
- loss of the extended family;
- differences in the ways our children behave; and
- changing community expectations of fathering.

Given that fathering is so obviously important, why are many dads not doing a good job of it? They obviously don't want to fail at it. In my talks with dads they gave four main reasons for not doing a great job:

'I never thought about it'

Most dads have never sat down and asked themselves what children really need – beyond the obvious (love, security) – so they don't know what to focus on when they are with their children.

'I had no idea what was really required of a dad'

Even if they do understand those needs, many fathers are not sure how to meet them. They base their fathering on things like common sense, their own experience as children and how their own father did the job. While quite a number of today's younger fathers read books and do parenting courses, many still resist the idea that they should step out and learn something about fathering.

'I was resistant to the idea of "learning" about fathering'

Some men have mental blocks that prevent them from developing their fathering skills. One of the saddest things during my interviews with men was that by the time they finally identified these blocks, it was too late to change anything – the children were already past the age when Dad could do anything other than apologise.

'I was always uncomfortable talking about personal stuff'

The men who would benefit most by reading this sort of stuff are the ones who are most likely to feel uncomfortable working through these issues. They are the ones most likely to say it is all 'bullshit'. Usually this attitude is a result of their own life experiences. Also, ironically, the very characteristics that have made men successful in their work can sometimes also create these mental blocks.

Work has changed

For most of human history Dad worked in or near the home, and children had plenty of access to him. Now Dad works away – in an office, factory, practice, truck, shop, etc. – and he is disconnected from his kids.

Also, there has been a shift from long-term careers to short-term, flexible, productivity-based jobs. This shift, combined with modern consumerism and unemployment, has removed a lot of the old job security and created a strong pressure to overwork.

Before the Industrial Revolution in Western Europe, people grew up in rural or village environments, and the children were around them all the time. Fathers would come and go from the house and children would help their parents with whatever had to be done. In those days, over 90 percent of people lived in farming communities – this has dropped to less than 5 percent now. Fathers have become largely absent from the fathering process only because of industrialisation. This means that it is not 'natural' for fathers to be absent from the fathering process – it is in fact a very 'unnatural' way of functioning.

It all changed with the Industrial Revolution, when dads suddenly started going off to work, away from home, for most of the day. This produced the 'factory father'. The 'factory' is now an office building, small business, construction site, shop, truck, hospital and so on, but the factory father is still there, getting up each morning and heading off to work, away from the family.

Many children now hardly ever spend time with their own fathers or father figures at kindergarten, or at school, or at the end of the school day when they go home or to after-school care.

Productivity-based work practices

There was a time, not long ago, when you could be almost guaranteed a job when you left school and, when you were in that job, you could stay there for the majority of your working life. Now there are many fewer long-term jobs. Many jobs that used to be carried out by the permanent staff of large companies are now contracted out and productivity is often considered more important than time spent at work now. Many of these workplace changes have been necessary but one can only hope that they are managed with compassion and sensitivity because they can precipitate longer working hours and a job insecurity which prevents people from relaxing enough to take the extra time with their children.

Long working hours are not just forced on us by our employers; they are also driven by our desire for money, security of tenure, approval, fame and power. This pressure can also come from the worker's partner, children and peers. The modern emphasis on consuming makes it worse, by creating a sense that we need things, when in fact we really just want them.

The effects

Leaving the home/village/tribe and going off to work in another place, a place where you are constantly under pressure and constantly insecure, is a very recent phenomenon. Indeed, if the whole of human history were reduced to just one day, the period of time when that has been the norm would be just 90 seconds. It is no wonder we haven't yet worked out how to manage the problems this setup has caused – problems for children, for fathers, for mothers, and for other adult carers.

Overall, these changes make it easy for us to overwork and harder for us to do our fathering well. Now dads tend to only see their children at the end of the day, the very time when dads – and kids! – are at their most tired. At the times of the day when dads are fresh and full of energy, the kids are miles away, at school or at home. On weekends or holidays dads often take a long time to recover, barely doing so before it is time to get stuck back into work again.

Women bear the brunt of the parenting in these situations, and they get tired of having to do their own share as well as most of their partner's share.

A strong fathering role is not an 'optional special treat' for children. It is an essential component of their development. If we are absent from their lives when they know we could be present, we are not giving them their best shot at developing as happy, healthy, well-balanced people.

Family structures have changed

Over the past 50 years or so we have begun to live in nuclear families, and thus have lost our best fathering resources – our extended family. They used to live with us or very close to us, and we used to be able to get on-the-spot advice on parenting from our brothers, cousins, father and uncles – whether we asked for it or not!

Children have also lost benefits they gained from the extended family structure. They used to be more able to seek alternative adults to talk to when they went through the normal process of realising they were separate people from their parents. Now, often, they can't. In a well-known example from 2000 years ago, it took three days before the parents of a twelve-year-old child, who was travelling home with his family group after visiting a major city, knew that he was missing. It was so commonplace to spend time and sleep over with relatives that it took a long time to notice he had been left back at the city. It is an example that shows that extended families had children moving around.

We now learn parenting on the job, by ourselves. We learn how to parent our first child by having our first child, and after having made all our 'first-child mistakes', we feel we know something about it. Trouble is, it is too late, because then we are on to our second child. We then learn how to be a parent to our second child and again, by the time we've learnt it, it's too late. By the time we have finished having children, we know lots about how to parent, but unfortunately, our knowledge can't be applied until the grandchildren arrive!

The absence of regular contact with a whole bunch of family members means that we make lots of otherwise avoidable mistakes; and by the time we realise we've made them, it is too late. The damage has been done. A number of fathers who were interviewed described this happening in their family, and said they wished they had had access to books on fathering that would have helped make up for the missing advice.

In old cultures the grandfather was there in the household and available to pass on fathering wisdom to his son. Now we have to learn by ourselves on the run. Maybe your book will help to replace the 'missing grandfather' because it has lots of advice from older men. Graham Barrett

We have to develop other ways to learn how to do a good job of fathering. It may be hard for us, as men, to accept that we need a bit of help in our fathering, but we do need to accept it. Of course extended families are not a perfect solution, and many generate strained relationships, but from a child's perspective there are many potential benefits, including a natural type of acceptance plus alternative adults to talk to.

Extended family for us is really important. In Perth we had no relatives. We had wonderful friends but they are not quite the same as relatives – you can lean on relatives more. Now that we are back in Melbourne we are in a big close family again and the kids have a lot of exposure to their uncles, aunts and cousins. Help is there without even asking for it and the kids experience a kind of relaxed acceptance with these uncles and aunts. It's hard to explain the benefits that an extended family provides children. I haven't really experienced it a lot myself as I am not as close to my extended family as Nanette has been to hers, but I believe the kids really do benefit from their relationships with the extended family. Michael Malthouse

It is often not possible to rekindle an extended family environment. Given that the nuclear family struggles when isolated, some form of community involvement becomes necessary.

The nuclear family doesn't work on its own, it doesn't have the richness. You need to choose where to live, and stay there, and invest in all kinds of networks so there are other people who love your kids too. Then you can be less than perfect, because you're part of a bigger whole. Steve Biddulph

Kids have changed

Each generation is a little different from the one before it, and there are many ways in which today's children are different from the way we were when we were children. If we don't appreciate that, we will miss the point in a lot of what we do with them.

A lot has been written about the huge range of choices that are available to children today, choices that were just not there in earlier days. This amount of choice has effects on today's kids – indecision, lack of commitment and confusion, at times. It's the same way we feel when we want to order a meal at a restaurant and are handed a menu with 50 different dishes on it.

You will have seen already that your children do not react the same way you did to a lot of things. They are less likely to commit time to ongoing groups such as scouts and summer sporting teams. They tend to avoid making early decisions, preferring to leave things to the last minute. These differences are not necessarily bad, they're just differences.

Society used to set the rules, and most followed them, but individual freedom is more valued now.

I think that young people today are very much an options generation. They don't make up their minds until the very end. They don't have any institutional loyalty. My generation had loyalty to a lot of organisations. My kids are very interested in sports, but they never want to tie themselves to playing the same thing every Saturday, and yet they want the option to do that. John Howard

We are less in a position to appeal to rules and authority and 'do what I tell you because I say so'-style parenting than our fathers ever were.

It is crucial to be aware of how things are different for our children compared with us, otherwise when they say 'but you just don't understand me', they will be right. In the words of one of the dads interviewed:

I don't think I am a good person to ask about fathering. Last week my fifteen-year-old daughter told me about her drug habit and my seventeen-

year-old son, who also does drugs, sat down and told me 'You've blown it as a father. You just don't understand. You were never there for me in those early teenage years when I really needed you.' It hit me in the guts. I'm still hurting over it. Maybe he's right. What do I do now?

Anonymous, travel agent

Society's expectations have changed

Over the past twenty years or so society's expectations of dads have changed. Findings from a recent survey showed that young men were beginning to view themselves as fathers first and workers second. More than 80 percent of young men said that a flexible schedule which gave them more family time was more important than money, power or prestige.

No longer is it enough for dads to be just breadwinners; we must also be playmates, nurturers, guides, entertainers, educators and counsellors – as we were before the Industrial Revolution. And we, as dads, have accepted these changes. We have different, higher expectations of ourselves.

Summary

- There are good and bad dads, and their children often know it.
- There is no 'ideal, model father' – everyone is different.
- Being a successful dad is not primarily about hours worked; it is about knowing what your children really need from you and responding to those needs.
- Good fathering is essential not just for children, but also for fathers.
- Modern trends towards short-term contracts and productivity-based work have combined with consumerism to increase the pressure on us to work long hours.
- The loss of the extended family means that men have lost a key resource for learning about and getting feedback on their fathering – their relatives.
- We need other strategies for learning about fathering.
- We need to make sure that women don't continue to be burdened with both mothering and fathering roles.
- Children are different today, so we can't base our fathering simply on our own experiences as children or on the fathering methods used by our dads.
- The community's expectations of fathers are much higher now than they were a generation ago.
- We put higher expectations on ourselves as fathers today.

IDEA FOR ACTION:

List the ways in which the social changes described in this chapter have impacted on you.

My advice to young men is don't get married too young and make sure you have access to all the good teaching stuff right from the beginning, such as books, courses, etc. Think about fathering early on so you don't find yourself parenting the same way your father did. Work hard to put whatever you learn into practice – old habits die hard, so you're going to have to work at it every day.   Peter de Blanc

I have had some fantastically powerful influences that have improved my fathering. The STEP course I did when my oldest child, Katie, was around ten was very helpful.   Peter Prout

Learn about fathering

Goals can only be reached if you learn the skills necessary to reach them. Willpower alone wouldn't get you to the summit of Everest. You need a plan. So it shouldn't be ridiculous to suggest that you would seek to improve your fathering skills. This could mean reading some books, attending some courses, discussing your goals with the children's mother and learning what you can from appropriate role models.

I suspect that the idea of learning about fathering won't really give working dads much of a shock. Most jobs require some sort of training and feedback, usually early in the job, as well as ongoing skill development. Nobody expects intuition to be enough in the workplace.

It is similar in golf – while intuition, natural talent and desire are enough to get you out on the course whacking golf balls around, and while some will naturally do better than others, in the end you won't get your score below a certain point. Errors – a bad slice, a hook, poor putting – will keep recurring, which will become frustrating. At that point the only way to improve is to have lessons and get feedback.

It amazes me how often intelligent men, who insist on the value of training, learning and feedback in their work, their sport and everything else they do, forget that the same principles apply to fathering. In their defence, though, when they are made aware of the inconsistency, most of them say they haven't deliberately taken that view, they simply have never really thought about it like that.

On a quick check of the Internet I found over 10,000 books and videos listed on how to improve your golf but less than 1 percent of that number on fathering. I guess it's easier to teach golf and to measure improvement in that. Books like this one are there to give some information and advice so that you can have it available from the early stages of fathering and, with any luck, avoid a lot of the mistakes that others have made. Most men I talk to about these ideas do quickly see their value.

I was highly resistant and refused to read any books or go to any courses. That was a mistake. If I had my time all over again I'd do it differently.

Allan Chapple

'Why can't I just do my fathering naturally – why do I need to read a book?'

A number of men insist that we should do our fathering by intuition and gut feeling. I strongly believe that this is just a current cultural view of fathering and is 'unnatural'. It is just a modern way of doing things – most of human history has been different. In the past many men had family/tribal behaviours to conform to, and spoken or written codes to follow. They were not free as dads to just 'go with the flow'. Is the old or new approach better? I think the old approach has a compelling logic to it. We are all strongly conditioned in some way or other by our life experiences, so it is hard to argue that our particular way of doing things is in any way really 'natural'.

The typical way of fathering in our culture is to wait for problems to occur then react to them. While that works for some things (every child will try to steal something, thereby creating an opportunity to teach them about things like integrity and respect), the reactive approach is not guaranteed to work for others e.g., drug-taking, sexuality issues, career planning and understanding their fears. What we need to do is shift from accepting what is *usual* in fathering to accepting only what is *good* in fathering.

A lot of dads have never thought much about learning any fathering skills

One of the most interesting things that happened during my interviews is that, although they were doing their best, many of these dads had not really thought about their fathering in terms of goals and evaluation of success, and most hadn't done much study of the subject. They had thought about everything else in life, but when it came to fathering they'd pretty much done it on the run, without seeking any information or advice.

Returning to the golf analogy – there is a huge difference between people who are naturally poor golfers and those who naturally have a lot of talent and take to the game easily, but most of us are somewhere in between. But virtually all golfers will benefit from lessons from a professional. In fact it's impossible to be an outstanding golfer without such lessons.

It's the same with fathering – no matter what level of ability you have, you can probably benefit from learning more. A number of the fathers I spoke to said at first that they had never learnt anything about fathering, they just did it on the run. But as they thought about it, they realised that they had unconsciously spent years watching friends who were fathers, trying to work out how fathers should behave. These fathers hadn't all refused to learn anything about fathering; they mostly hadn't been exposed to any information, and had no peers who talked about such things, or it had just never really crossed their minds.

Some dads don't want to develop their fathering skills

There were some fathers who said they had had a great resistance to learning about fathering in their early fathering years (often when it had been mentioned to them by their wives!), which they later regretted. Others had other blocks.

Just identifying these blocks is usually enough to begin to overcome them.

Some of the main blocks described by dads are related to:

- Having fixed ways of fathering.
- Believing that fathering should be natural and intuitive, not learnt or planned.
- Feeling that fathering should be easy, and that books on fathering just make it all sound like hard work, like an extension of the working day.
- Being fooled by a false notion of quality time.
- Being more focused on the 'product' (future adult) than the 'process' (enjoying being a dad).
- Not believing that fathering makes any great difference to life outcomes for your children.
- Fear of hypocrisy – telling children not to do something that you got away with when you were their age.
- Lacking confidence in being a father.
- Unconsciously acting like your own father.
- Consciously acting like your own father.

Or to people's tendency to react to 'personal' stuff:

- Feeling uncomfortable with anything that sounds like life skills, the inner self or sensitive New Age, 'touchy-feely psychobabble'.
- Avoiding the issue of the need to change aspects of your fathering style (this is the old 'ABC' problem – 'Avoidance Blocks Change').
- Rejecting advice because you don't understand it.
- Using the two 'great escape' strategies ('This is all bullshit', and 'I'm not comfortable with this').
- Wanting to avoid feeling vulnerable about the children.
- Blocked communication generally.
- Resisting change of any sort, on principle.
- Being unwilling to take responsibility for mistakes ('the blame reflex').

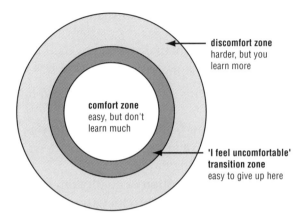

Or to the busyness of our working lives:

- Forgetting *why* we are really working (for our families and for fun, meaning and competition, not for money, power and glory).
- Postponing commitment to good fathering until too late.

Or to our *style* of working:

- Having a 'narrow window' between stress and boredom.
- Staying in task-oriented mode after leaving work.
- Not leaving the need to 'remain in control' at work.
- Being a lecturer, not a listener.
- Being fooled by the lack of instant rewards in fathering.
- Being a perfectionist – not ever being able to let the children have messy rooms, etc.
- Being inflexible about home schedules.
- Having difficulty relaxing long enough to have fun.

Or to letting our own needs and reactions get in the way:

- Allowing work to become a 'mistress' (giving us nice feedback, making us feel special and taking us away from the family).
- Forgetting *who* we are working for – we work for our family, not for our boss: he or she will never love us as much as our families do, no matter how hard we work!
- Being too proud to apologise to children when you make a mistake.

Keep an open mind about the possibility of changing how you do things. Not wanting to change the way you do something is quite normal for humans. The longer we have done things a particular way the less likely it is that we will even consider that there is another way to do things that might be more effective. This has nothing to do with intelligence. Let me illustrate this point by describing an experience I had when I first joined the medical school.

When I started teaching medical students, I taught the way I thought you should teach, largely following what my own teachers had done. Most of the other teachers did the same. Then a couple of interesting things happened.

Firstly, we started getting much more detailed student evaluation of our lectures, and it turned out that no matter how hard we tried and how entertaining the lectures were, students found that lectures weren't the best way to learn. They were mostly learning better by other methods. It became clear that a lot of our lectures were actually almost a waste of everyone's time, even though they were 'good' lectures. Unfortunately, because we ourselves were all taught by lectures, we were incredibly resistant to stopping our lectures, despite strong evidence that we needed to change this teaching method.

Secondly, we had some professional educators work with us. Just having them there, asking us questions like 'How do students learn best?' rather than 'How can you improve your lectures?' made us realise, fairly quickly, that we hadn't really thought it through. What interested me was the way that outside, objective information helped me question:

- the way I did things;
- my own resistance to change;
- my strong conviction that I was doing the right thing; and
- my desire to continue using the same methods I had used in the past.

The other lecturers had the same reactions. Since then we have all, however reluctantly, made dramatic changes to the way we teach medical students and we are doing a far better job of it, based on current student evaluation.

I've noticed it's the same for fathering. No matter how well you are doing the job of fathering, some form of input and evaluation, combined with a willingness to change, can have a profound effect. I described in the Introduction the false notion that 'active fathering is a modern fad', and pointed out that it is, in fact, the opposite – it is only in recent times, and mostly in affluent countries, that fathers have not had to learn about fathering, be accountable for it and be heavily involved in it. In times past, fathers generally took an active role in the process of bringing up children. They had a code of behaviour and a corporate way of encouraging that behaviour.

Circumstances affect your fathering

The increase in the number of women in the paid workforce has forced many fathers to stop functioning on automatic pilot, and sit down and talk to their partners to discuss what it is their children need from them, how they can give them those things, and how they can work together to manage the house and their work, and still get time for the children. Men in this situation are lucky: they have been awakened to their fathering role before they just charged off and did the same things as their own dads, making assumptions about fathering and taking it for granted.

Dad never darkened the door of the school when I was a kid, so why am I here today? What happened was that my wife was working too, and we had to sit down and discuss our roles. It can be a problem for me sometimes too, this changing roles. I've got to keep working to get used to it. I think dads ought to share all the parenting roles. I really enjoy it, although honestly I still think the mothers do it better.

Anonymous (comments made at school orientation day)

Sometimes it is divorce that forces men to overcome their block. When they separate, some men start to spend different time with the children – for the first time, they may be required to take them to school and to know what is going on there. In the process, they are forced to think more about the process of parenting, and some realise, sometimes too late, what they have missed out on.

I didn't have much to do with the kids initially. Basically I went to work, came home and went to work again. I had three daughters and I knew nothing about their schooling or anything else. My dad was never involved in my schooling and I guess I just followed his example. Then my marriage split up and I had the children for three days of the week and I just had to do it. I've realised that I enjoy it, so today both I and my ex-wife are here with our current spouses, even though I don't need to be here.

The truth is that I was forced to spend this extra time with my girls and I really enjoyed it. I've ended up with a better relationship with them than if we had never got divorced and I'd continued with my hectic work schedules. Of course it's not good that we got divorced, but it has awakened me to this part of my life. I wish I had done it earlier.

Anonymous (comments made at school orientation day)

'Can good fathering really be learnt? Aren't we just wired to be who we are?'

In everything in life the attitude that what you start with will determine whether or not you learn anything. As the famous saying goes, 'If you think you can, or if you think you can't, you're right.'

Almost everything in life is a mixture of our genes plus our environment – 'nature plus nurture'. That applies to things like cancer, intelligence, depression, heart disease, alcoholism and other behaviours. Your genes never make you do anything. It is the same for your children – there is no doubt that the genes they are born with will affect their personalities, but how they are treated while they are growing up will determine, to a large extent, how their personalities are expressed. As we said about golf, there are not many people would not benefit from some extra input and feedback. It might be a bit uncomfortable at first, and it may take a little while to improve, and even longer before you start to enjoy it more.

Most dads probably do at least an okay job of fathering, and reading a book like this and following some of the suggestions could help almost all readers.

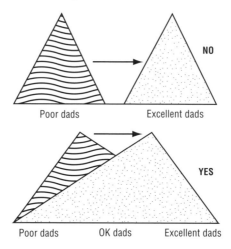

A book like this won't miraculously turn us all into excellent dads, but we could all be helped a bit. A small number will find that a book like this dramatically changes the way they father.

There are dads who will never change at all. There are those who are already fantastic fathers, who would not learn anything new reading this book. They are rare. No *perfect* dads exist. Men who seriously want to be better dads will always find something helpful in a book like this and will want to get others to read it.

Then there are fathers who could improve but never will, either because they don't want to change or because they have a fear of failing which prevents commitment, so they won't try. They are also rare. Where do you think you fit in to this graph, and how open to change are you?

It's a pity it's too late to apply what I have learnt about fathering. I wish I could do it all over again. Allan Chapple

We learn how to be parents on the job, but we do not really graduate with a diploma in parenting until the children are adults and it is too late.

Grandparents can be mellow, because it is their second shot at it and they can use all the wisdom that they have gained over the years.

Michael Chaney

I have emphasised the need to learn fathering skills because I have met such strong resistance to it in some men – I felt it needed a fair bit of discussion.

Learning about fathering from books

Having community 'fathering codes' to learn from is not a recent invention. In the ancient Jewish literature the Hebrew fathers wandering in the desert were exhorted to read their tribal law to their children each day at meal times and when walking with them, and to encourage each other in this activity (Deuteronomy 6:7). Muslim teaching in the Koran contains instructions to fathers to provide for their children and show them affection (the Koran *2:253*). Christian teaching is similar, with fathers exhorted to love their children, to teach them and to be an example to them of love and humility (Ephesians 3:21, Colossians 3:12–20).

'Code of behaviour' wisdom was also passed down by elders in tribal cultures. Virtually all cultures in the past had, and many today have, a code and rituals involving the clear instruction of children as they pass from childhood to adulthood. What follows from this is that learning about fathering is a core element of human life. Books just replace other sources of learning that no longer have a central role in our modern society – written codes, extended family living and tribal elders.

In my generation we used to read Dr Spock. We read the book and we discussed it. I never did a course on parenting, and mostly otherwise learnt from trial and error and observing the mistakes of others.   Peter Carnley

There are some excellent books available about fathering, parenting, manhood and specific issues.

Chris took on his fathering with guts. He resented not having the time to spend with the kids that he wanted to, but during the last few years he took to reading inspirational books that would help him make the most of the opportunities that were sent his way. One of his favourite books was Manhood, *by Steve Biddulph. In fact he wanted to go to one of Steve's talks, but we only ever found out he was in Perth when it was too late. A book about busy fathers would be one that I know Chris would have invested his time in reading, and it took no time at all for Mel and Trenton to decide that they would like to contribute their eulogies if it helps another dad to learn how to be as special as theirs was. They are as excited as I am about the prospect that at least something good can come out of this mess. Chris spent a lot of time talking to other men in the recent past about the importance of making the most of the time you had with your family. Thank you for the opportunity for Mel and Trenton to tell the world about their dad.*
Love Gillian

Gillian Beale

Note: Mel and Trenton's comments about their dad and his fathering were read as eulogies at his funeral and are included elsewhere in the book.

Blokes will read words of advice, but they won't like to read too much theory.

Graham Barrett

I've learnt a bit about fathering from reading. I guess that's partly related to my job. It's been extremely helpful, and I would encourage young fathers to read books about fathering so that they learn early on what to do, and avoid just doing what their dads did.

Ray Arthur

I read a book called P.E.T. (Parent Effectiveness Training). It's a bit American, but, by golly, it makes a lot of sense to me; and since reading it and applying the message, things have got a lot better here.

Ben Timmis

Mostly it is wives who recommend that the men read the book Manhood. *Although I have read a lot about parenting, American self-help books have not been helpful ... mostly they do not fit with my own experience. The Australian books on the subject make their points more clearly.*

Glenn Begley

I have also learnt a lot from my mistakes. I didn't read much or have any exposure to any parenting courses – that sort of information wasn't really available out in the bush.

Harry Perkins

Other things I learnt from were books such as Fatherhood *by Bill Cosby and* The Seven Habits of Highly Effective Families *by Steve Covey, as well as from friends, because I'd watched the way they'd parented their kids. I also learnt a lot about parenting from the Bible, from the rules and examples there.*

Peter de Blanc

I've read Steve Biddulph's book and I've also read The Two-Minute Father. *A lot of it is stuff that I knew already from my job as a preacher ...*

Tim Costello

Some men never read, so for them to learn from books about fathering they might need to get together with other men who have read these sorts of books and talk about the issues.

I never read any books about fathering but then I have only read about six books in my whole life. But I am enjoying talking about it with you now, so I will read your book.

Greg Wade

Fathering courses

Most of the men I interviewed had not attended any fathering course; some, who had been too busy to attend themselves, had listened to what their wives had to say when they returned from such courses.

I never did any course on parenting ... Cailey tends to read all these books and pass information on to me.

Kanishka Raffel

Merrin did the parenting courses – I was too busy working. I guess that is the common experience.

Glenn Begley

Most of the men that come to my seminars are dragged there by their wives. You can see the heel marks in the carpet outside the entrance door! When they do come and listen they get annoyed with themselves because they realise they should have thought about doing this sort of stuff before.

Anonymous, parenthood lecturer

I wish I had done some training, because with parenting the ground keeps moving. You have to keep learning all the time because it's not long before your kids move into a new stage and you've got to learn it all over again. Parents easily get stuck in the previous stage and are always playing 'catch up'. Getting some training would probably help anticipate what's coming.

Allan Chapple

However, several of the men said that going to such a course had had a profound effect on their fathering, especially Parent Effectiveness Training (PET) and Systematic Training for Effective Parenting (STEP) courses. My wife and I had great fun after we attended a STEP parenting course, coming home and telling our children what we had learnt, asking them whether or not we were already doing it, and where we needed to improve. I do not know how good the feedback was, but at least the children were aware that we took our parenting seriously and wanted to do a good job.

Courses have two main advantages: they give you the accumulated wisdom of years of study, observation and research by many people: they give you an opportunity to sit around talking to other parents, and to realise that the difficulties you are having with your children are common to most parents.

It is useful to be able to talk about these problems with others.

I learnt a lot from three years of training in marriage and family counselling at Kinway. That particularly helped me allow for children's individuality and avoid laying my own expectations on them.

Harley Hayward

We all did a personal development course called Forum, and my relationship with my daughter, and our family relationships in general, improved a lot. Brian Smith

I did a parenting course early on and I found it very helpful. It made me think a lot about things. In fact I believe that courses are good in almost everything you do in life – you can only get better. Geoff Creelman

These courses are not 'magic fixes' – they are just useful launching pads for change.

I was a single father (sole parent) for some twelve years, beginning when my children were six and one. It was a challenging time. I would have to get up at 5 a.m. to fit in the domestic duties, including washing school uniforms, having lunches ready and basically foreseeing their requirements for the day ahead. When the kids were about ten and five I spoke to a teacher who recommended that I do a Parent Effectiveness Training course. I was a bit sensitive about criticism and thought, 'what right has a teacher to imply that I was not doing a good job as a father!' I went along to the course and felt very self-conscious, because I was the only dad amongst approximately ten mothers. However, I found the course was a great help. I heard other people talking about the problems that they had with their children. The problems were very similar to my own and I learnt how to share my personal experiences in bringing up children. I realised you don't have to battle along by yourself and it is okay to talk about it. Since then I have never been particularly self-conscious in talking about those personal issues. I think women are much better about addressing these types of personal issues and talking about it than men are, in general. Richard Court

We've done PET and STEP as well as some personal and family counselling courses. These have been important because they have challenged my thought patterns and the behaviour patterns in my parenting.

Peter de Blanc

It is a good idea to try more than one way of learning about fathering.

Although I have read books, I'm really someone who seeks lots of types of input rather than just one bit of input, like listening to other dads.

Ian Robinson

Summary

■ Willpower alone won't make you a great dad.

■ Many dads have never thought much about learning any fathering skills, and some resist even the idea of learning about fathering.

■ Men forced by circumstances to think more about fathering often realise what they have been missing.

■ Good fathering can be learnt: many fathers have found books and courses on fathering very valuable.

■ Fathering books and courses are not 'magic fixes' – they are just a jumping-off point for change.

■ It's a good idea to try more than one way of learning about fathering.

 IDEA FOR ACTION

Discuss with your partner or a friend which of the mental blocks listed in this chapter apply to you and what you might do to get around them. Read at least one other book on fathering/parenting.

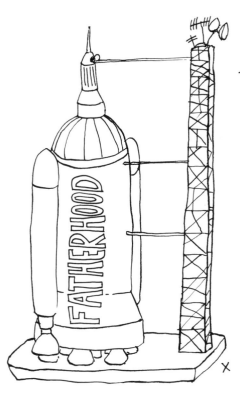

☆ BASE TO BOB,
  COME IN BOB,
  OVER...

⚡ BOB TO BASE,
  I READ YOU, OVER...

☆ BASE TO BOB,
  WE'RE COMMENCING
  COUNTDOWN...
  THIS IS WHEN ALL
  THAT TRAINING
  FINALLY PAYS OFF!
  OVER...

☆ BASE TO BOB?
  DO YOU COPY?
  OVER...

⚡ BOB TO BASE...
  UM...
  WHAT TRAINING?
  OVER...

I do not really know how to evaluate my role and my success as a father. However, I look at the boys and am very happy and proud of them as they are now, so perhaps they have received some good fathering. I have no doubt they have received good mothering. I am proud of what they are like, how well they relate to their peers and their parents, what they think about and how much I just enjoy them as people.

Glenn Begley

If my children read this in the future, I guess I would tell them that I wish I could have been a better father and spent more time with them and been more supportive of them, but then we have a wonderful relationship with each of them and they have turned out to be good people, so maybe the parenting has been okay.

Michael Chaney

Evaluate fathering

'How will I know if my fathering strategy is working?'

If you try to improve your golf you get regular feedback – every weekend you have to mark your scorecard! Many things in life are like that. How do you know whether you're doing a good job as a father, though?

It seems a very important question, but an answer is very difficult to find. There are many standards people use to get some idea – from others – about how they are doing. It is a difficult area, largely because the personality of the parent, the child or the independent observer will all profoundly influence how the evaluation comes out.

What are the opinions of your children?

Of course you can't ask your children when they are young, because young children, if they don't get their own way, will all say that you don't do anything for them. Teenagers by definition think their fathers – and their mothers, and most other adults! – are lepers and know nothing. It's only when your children become young adults and have to parent children themselves that they realise what sort of a job you've done.

It's difficult to know how effective you have been as a parent, particularly when they are going through a rebellious stage. You need to appreciate that it is just a phase and not necessarily your fault. They know they may be causing problems. It is important that at all times you are there to help them through it, and that's where unconditional love becomes critical.

Richard Court

My children are adults now, and I guess I evaluate my parenting based on what they tell me now. They are very quick to tell me whether I have been relevant or not. I guess I would be worried if they ever stopped talking to me, but they have never done that – they have always continued to maintain open communication. Harry Perkins

As the kids have got older I have listened to what they say about my fathering. For example my oldest daughter, Kate, is living in Canada, and she has put down in letters her feelings about my fathering. She says, for example, 'How did you put up with all the things that I did?' Peter Prout

The best way to evaluate whether or not you were a good father, I think, is whether or not the children really want to be with you. Do they like to spend time with you, or would they rather be somewhere else?

Peter Prout

The trouble is, if we wait until they are adults it is a bit late to change anything. If they tell you then what you could have done better, it's pretty much too late to change. It would be more helpful to have had feedback on the job.

What is your children's mother's opinion?

Asking your partner is not a bad idea, but some partners tend to be critical and some are accepting, and it is hard for any father to completely meet the expectations of his partner. Partners come into any relationship with surprisingly fixed expectations of each other. Men have a concrete view of fathering that generates their expectations of their own performance as dads. They also have a preconceived view of what mothering should be. These views are usually generated from their own experience of family (things they wish to either emulate or avoid). Similarly, women come into relationships with different views of mothering and fathering. These differences will be found in every area of parenting, including discipline, beliefs, handling emotions and learning styles. Understanding these different expectations, discussing differences and where they come from and agreeing to a continual process of review, learning and change are more likely to produce results than just trying to meet your partner's expectations of you.

Getting opinions from third parties

You can ask a third party, someone outside your family – they can often see lots of things that you might not see.

You only know you have been a good dad when you get feedback about your own kids from other people – that they are nice children, that they relate well to everybody else, that they are well-mannered, etc. You can never know about those things if you base your opinions on their behaviour at home!
Geoff Marsh

What is your own judgement of your performance?

You can ask yourself. However, some of us tend to be self-critical. If only we had a fathering scorecard like golf to help us know where we stand.

Some fathers can be overcritical of themselves.

I don't tend to trust my own judgement on whether I am a good father. It is hard to evaluate your own fathering. Because my own father always put me down and made me think I was incompetent, I always have a tendency to criticise myself. The trouble with that is that it takes the focus off the children and puts it onto me. I can't trust my own judgement because I will be too hard on myself.   Peter Prout

Evaluation can be pretty subjective. In my observation dads who do a really good job tend to knock themselves a bit and fathers who aren't doing such a great job often feel self-satisfied. I don't know why that is.

It is the same with competence in the workplace. The best people are the ones who seek counsel; the worst don't know how bad they are and what they need.   Ian Robinson

Self-evaluation of your success as a father is very difficult.

I do not ever tend to think about what I would do better if I had my time all over again. I do not ever tend to dwell on the past – I am pretty much always someone who looks at the future. I believe we should make the most of our opportunities, live with the decisions we have made and move on instead of agonising over them all the time.   Glenn Begley

Don't expect to know for sure whether you are doing a good job as a parent. If you worry and think about your kids you'll probably end up doing the right thing, but you will not have the luxury of knowing that at the time.   M. Scott Peck

I think it's almost impossible to evaluate whether you're doing a good job as a father. There are plenty of terrific fathers whose children become drug addicts or commit suicide. Family is central, but kids can always fall foul of other relationships, particularly when they get older. Then the pull of those other relationships becomes stronger than the family. You can only do so much as a father. Kim Beazley

How have your kids turned out?

It is important to remember that the way the children turn out is strongly influenced by the input they receive from each parent, but that is not the only input they get. In other words you can do the best job in the world as a father or a mother and the children might still end up having problems – inevitably lots of things work together to influence how a child turns out. Therefore there is value in looking at the 'product' for your answers, but that value is limited.

Judging by your kids' performance

It's hard to evaluate your fathering. Part of this is done on outcomes, and I'm pleased to say that both the boys are doing well academically.
Geoff Gallop

I guess I feel really great about my kids' achievements. Melissa is a state basketballer and Shaun is a state cricketer. Geoff Marsh

I have succeeded as a dad if they make a contribution to society.
Mark Edwards

Judging by how your kids relate to people

I feel I've done a good job as a father if my children relate well to others and give themselves to other people. Ray Arthur

But it is not just sports. About three weeks ago, Melissa had some friends over and I looked at those children, such a wonderful group of children, and I felt very proud. I guess it is because I realised they knew how to be happy and to choose good friends. Geoff Marsh

It's also about how well they relate, and they are both settled well in their relationships with their friends, their relationship with adults and their relationship to me. Also, they think their own thoughts and have their own views on things and are well balanced. But in the end I think you never really know.   Geoff Gallop

I don't know how to evaluate whether I'm being a good dad or not. Sometimes I think you will never know. If you're lucky you might get a nanosecond of feedback on your deathbed. Really, though, I think if they're getting on with their peers and relating well then you've done a good job as a dad.   Tony Cooke

Judging by your kids' behaviour, attitudes and values

I evaluate my success as a father on the behaviour, attitudes and values of my children as I observe them in their relationships with their friends, in their schooling and how others react to them. It is also how they react to adversity – my daughter Alison will be in the Olympic trials this weekend, and will probably miss out because she hasn't been performing well. She will be sad for a while but then she will get over it quickly and get on with life. That kind of attitude makes me realise that I have probably done an okay job in my fathering.   John Inverarity

I tend to evaluate my fathering based on the children's reactions to things that I do. For example, recently we had an issue of behaviour with the girls, when they were at the beach cottage. They wanted to do something I was against, so we sat them down around the table with a glass of wine and spent an hour discussing it. They complained about the restrictive rules I was setting, so I invited them to go away and write out their own set of rules. They came back with some written rules that we then agreed to modify, because they were a bit unreasonable, and then we finally *agreed to a set of rules. As I drove home from the beach cottage with them, I felt satisfied that I had done a good job of fathering in that situation.* Anonymous, businessman

Judging by how well your children relate to you

The relationship that children develop with their parents when they become adults is a complex issue. For some families that might involve continuing to work together, whereas for others it might mean being scattered across the world. There is no simple formula that describes 'success as a parent' when these relationships are considered – except, of course, that you are still in a relationship rather than not communicating at all.

Although I have been really busy, I think my giving all of my spare time to my family has been successful, because we have remained very close. Whether the boys are in New York or Sydney, we still call each other most days and chat. Ian Constable

You did okay as a dad if they like being in a relationship with you after they don't need to be. If they remain affectionate and express happiness and fun with you then you have been successful. Allan Chapple

I don't believe you can really know while you're a father whether you're doing a good job, only on reflection. Probably if the kids like to be with you and engage with you that's a good sign. Peter de Blanc

I think you know that you are doing a good job as a dad if the kids still want to be with you and go places with you no matter what has happened in all of our lives. Another clue to our success is that the kids have always wanted us to join them at their parties, at a stage when other kids didn't want their parents around. Brian Edwards

You know you're okay as a father when they volunteer to say anything about their lives – what they are doing, what's on their mind and so on. Ian Robinson

I think it's quite easy to know whether you're doing a good job as a dad. It's whether your kids talk to you when they've got problems, whether they listen to you and whether they like your company. Peter Le Soeuf

I guess one sign that I may have done a good job is that my son prefers to come to the football with his dad, not with his mates.

Harry Perkins

I guess I feel I have succeeded if the kids miss me when I am not here and if they are affectionate towards me when I am here.   Paul Bannan

It's hard to know if you are doing a good job as a dad. I think if they show you affection back again, you are.   Craig Serjeant

I have succeeded as father if the kids are happy and if they have respect for other people.   Mark Edwards

Last week my fifteen-year-old daughter hugged me at school in front of all the other kids and wasn't embarrassed. The other parents were amazed that I have a daughter who is happy to do that.   Peter Prout

Judging by whether or not you remain 'connected' to your kids as they grow up

I evaluate my fathering based on whether or not I am connected with my children. If I feel unconnected then I feel I am failing. If I feel I am connected then I am doing well.   Murray Green

You know when you're doing a good job with your kids when you really feel connected to them, you know what's going on and they like to be with you. The time to watch out is if you feel these moments of connectedness are starting to fade. If that happens, stop and take a good look at yourself.   Peter de Blanc

Judging by whether or not your kids feel free to criticise or joke with you

Strangely, one mark of success at the time is if your teenagers feel secure enough to criticise you and let all the spew out. It doesn't feel good at the time, but it shows that they know that they don't have to fear rejection – which is why they're on their best behaviour at other people's places! Probably the teenagers themselves aren't aware of a lot of this at the time. I don't think this is just a false way of comforting myself for those terrible years. Really it is impossible to know how well you are doing when you are parenting adolescents.   Allan Chapple

When I get too busy the kids notice it. The other night I came home and found a note from my sixteen-year-old son, Tim, telling me I obviously didn't care much about him any more. I was clearly just not interested. I thought about it for a while and realised that his criticism was correct – my altered behaviour had affected him a lot, and I just hadn't realised it. I read the note and then walked into his room and gave him a big hug and said, 'Mate. That's a fair cop. I'm sorry.' Craig Serjeant

When families are close and the kids have a relationship with their parents it is a bit like being a friend. They can, if they have that tendency, be really rude. In families where the father is more austere and distant this doesn't happen, but as a father I've had to learn not to overreact to my kids, particularly my son, if he is rude to me. For example in the past he has said things like 'You are a dickhead' or 'F*** off'. If you told me when I started fathering that I was going to have to listen to that I would have said that I would not put up with it. But it is crucial not to overreact, and in fact he and I are really close. I know other fathers have that problem, too.

Anonymous, doctor

If you're close to your kids they will have a convivial go at you.

John Howard

How they relate to me is a difficult one. There will likely be three to four years when they will hate my guts. If they say to me at that time, 'Dad, you give me the shits' or, 'You didn't spend enough time with us' then that will be a good sign. If they feel free to say that sort of thing to me, then I'll think I've probably done a good job. If they do, I will sit down and say, 'Let's discuss what you've said, whenever you are ready to discuss it.' If they 'own me' in public when they are fifteen, I will be over the moon. Tony Cooke

An unclassifiable evaluation!

The kids are a bit young so it's hard to know if I'm doing a good job as a dad. Recently we were on holidays down in Augusta and I looked out and saw the two girls skipping and playing, with the blue sky and the trees around them and it was a beautiful sight. In fact I felt it was too beautiful to look at, and I felt inadequate. I felt I didn't deserve them. These girls were too precious a thing to be a steward of. Feeling such love I guess I can't have messed up my job completely. Kanishka Raffel

Overall in the interviews, each dad chose a slightly different way of evaluating their own fathering. They judged it by:

- their kids' performance;
- their kids' relationships with others;
- the freedom their children felt to criticise their parents;
- feedback from their children;
- their kids' behaviour, attitudes and values; or
- a combination of the above.

The fact that dads gave such varied answers is a reminder that this is not a clear area at all. Each father will have to find his way through the self-evaluation minefield, and different ways of judging the success – or otherwise – of our fathering will feel right at different times. The point is that we need to at least think, all the time, about whether or not we are doing a good job, and about how we will know that.

Summary

- It is very hard to know how well we are doing as fathers.

- The opinions of our children, their mother or others are helpful, but not final.

- Self-reporting is useful, but remember the personality of the father concerned: overcritical dads will devalue themselves, and vice versa.

- Evaluation on the basis of the kids' academic performance is of limited value.

- How your children relate to people is a good method of evaluation.

- Feedback from your children is more helpful as they get older.

- How your children behave, and their attitudes and values, is a popular method of evaluation: 'if they relate well to you, you are doing a good job' was the most common response from the dads I interviewed.

- If the children feel free to criticise or joke with their fathers, it is a good sign, not a bad one.

 IDEA FOR ACTION

Ask you children's mother which areas of fathering she feels you are doing well in and which areas need a bit of attention.

OK Dad. Your fathering since last meeting has been good. Cuddles, plays and trips to the park are all up. This is encouraging. We've noticed shoulder rides and bath-times are down, not really a cause for concern, but I'll flag it anyway. Now, about pocket-money...

When the children were very young I was working very hard and was a bit ambitious. I sat down and asked myself, 'Is work my main priority, or are my children my priority?' I thought about going higher and higher in the education system, even daydreamed about becoming Director General of Education, then looked at my children. I'm no saint, and my wife had to remind me of the importance of the decision, but in the end it had to be my decision. I chose to make my children my first priority. I spent as much time as I could with them. We

did lots of things together and I have enjoyed them immensely. I was always there for them and now, with this diagnosis of cancer, I can sit here and honestly say that there is nothing I feel I haven't done that I should have done with them. I made the right decision way back then.

Tony Weller

Another motivating factor for me in my fathering is that I lost my own dad when I was nine. He died in an Air India plane crash flying out of New Delhi. I missed out on learning practical things, like how to change a fuse. I also missed out on being a mate with my dad. I especially noticed this around

the age of eighteen when I saw a lot of my friends becoming mates with their dads. I want to be there for that. My greatest fear is dying, but not for me — for Josh and Sophie. For example, I have decided to get fit because I don't want to die of a heart attack, as I have been a bit overweight lately.

John Dickson

Chapter 12

Don't take fathering for granted

- Why every fathering moment is precious
- Choosing the right work–fathering balance
- Staying on track with your fathering

What is going to motivate a busy dad to change his work habits? Even if you read this book and get motivated in your fathering, within hours you can be swamped by the priorities of work again. This chapter is for those dads who need a bit of a reality check to make them wake up and focus on their children.

Many of the fathers interviewed in this book regretted having worked too hard or simply failed to focus enough on their children, taking time with them for granted. They hadn't worried enough about the future and, in retrospect, they wished they had woken up earlier to the opportunities they had to spend time with their children.

If you appreciate how precious time is, and the fact that neither you nor your children has a guarantee of lots of it, you can sort out the things that you really want to do as a father. We all need a certain amount of anxiety to remind us of the preciousness of time, and of the fact that it is always running out.

Pushed too far, though, anxiety can create a phobic, neurotic fear for our children. It can cause us to try to control them and their lives too much. This can produce possessiveness and a level of anxiety that the children absorb, putting them at risk of becoming anxious and of feeling that the world is an intrinsically unsafe place, which it is not. It is important in fathering, as in other things, to know how much is too little and how much is too much.

Taking kids for granted

If something is 'good for you' there is a tendency to imagine that the more you have of it, the more it helps you. This is not the case. One of the things you notice as soon as you start studying medicine is the frequent presence of a clearly defined biological 'bell curve' – there is an amount of something which is not enough, there is an amount that is optimal, and more than that amount is not always better. In other words, too little of something will not achieve a successful outcome, while too much can prevent a successful outcome. The trick is to find the amount that is 'just right'.

An obvious example is food. Too little means starvation, but too much leads to obesity, which itself causes all sorts of health problems. Optimal health requires an *appropriate* amount of food. It's the same for drugs. Too little will not achieve its desired effect, but too much can cause toxic side-effects. You've got to get the amount just right for a successful outcome. This bell curve applies to hundreds of thousands of biological molecules and processes in the human body.

A bell curve in fathering applies to the optimal amount of anxiety needed to keep our fathering at the right level. Too little anxiety creates a kind of distant, indifferent, blasé attitude to raising children, the feeling that time goes on forever and 'I can do my fathering stuff tomorrow.' It means taking time for granted.

The 'How to avoid taking kids for granted' anxiety bell curve

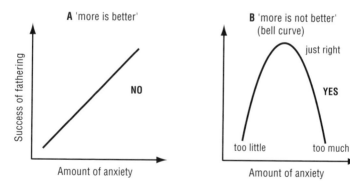

My best bit of advice for dads comes from the Bible and says 'Don't exasperate your kids.' You can exasperate your kids if you do too little for them, if you ignore them, or if you do too much for them and try to control them or nag them. Getting that balance is what I think the phrase 'Don't exasperate your kids' really means.   Peter Chappell

Sometimes we need a bit of a nudge to rearrange our priorities and stop taking time with our children for granted.

There is no guarantee that we will live long enough to see our kids grow up

I make no apologies for reminding you that you may, at any time, get the bad news that you will not live to see your children grow up. I have seen it often in my work. If my saying that reminds you of the preciousness of the time you spend with your children, and helps push you along the bell curve to the point where you are as good a father as you can be, it is justified.

Reality checks stop us taking things for granted. How many times have you been speeding down the road and noticed a white cross on the side of the road indicating that it is a point at which someone has died in a traffic accident? I slow down at such places.

I used to experience the same thing as a medical student and intern when I attended the emergency department and saw the victims of traffic accidents. It was an enormous reality check for us and we always drove home extremely carefully after such experiences.

I get reality checks every week in my job. It's a favour that medicine has done for me in my life – it has always helped me keep things in perspective. You may have had a reality check yourself when a friend or acquaintance has died.

The lesson applies to fathering just as it does to everything else. You have to realise that you may not actually have as much time as you thought. That is a really useful realisation, and should help you get your life's priorities right. A useful rule of thumb may be to try to live as though something bad just might happen to you tomorrow, so you'd better make the most of your time now, today. If you learn to live with this attitude, if you do get a bad diagnosis from your doctor, you will be able to say that you regret nothing, and you know there isn't anything you've left unsaid or undone with your children.

> During the Columbine High School massacre, business teacher Dave Sanders lay bleeding to death in a locked classroom. 'I can't breathe,' he murmured. 'I've got to go.' But the students kept talking to him. In a desperate effort to keep him going they pulled his wallet out of his pocket and held up the pictures of his daughters. As a last desperate measure they called upon the thing that would be most important to him as a dad – pictures of his daughters. 'Tell us about them,' they said.
>
> Time Magazine

Think about that. For all dads, their children are the most valued things in their lives. I don't want to sound overly morbid, but saying goodbye to them is something I see men having to do all the time. Men do die, and they do leave children behind.

Getting cancer has been a reality check for us. We had both been very heavily involved with work and had senior jobs in Canberra, but since my diagnosis we have quit work and just enjoyed life. We have begun to notice that the sky is blue, and we have enjoyed being able to get up in the morning and have morning tea together. We have loved being able to spend time with the children, helping them with their jobs, moving house etc. Everyone needs reality checks in life. Ross and Vanessa Divett

Those who suffer are those who are left behind, and it is crucial that children feel as though they've had their fair share of Dad. Your time with them is an investment that, if you do die, gives them the inner resources to get on with life.

Rebecca said she treasured her morning walk along the beach to Peter's Pool with her father. Andrew, aged seventeen, said he was a close friend of his dad's. He had looked forward to Friday evenings when he could spend some time with him.

Eulogies by children of shark attack victim, Ken Crew

If you were to die suddenly, would your children have that rich treasure chest of memories with you that, while it would cause them initial grief, would sustain them for the rest of their lives? I was recently reminded of this when I attended the funeral of Chris Beale, a cousin of mine – a wonderful, kind man with a great sense of humour who loved his children to bits and did a lot of things with them. He died suddenly of an unexpected illness. The words of his children's eulogies from his funeral service have kindly been made available to me, and are reproduced in various places in this book.

There are no guarantees that our kids will live to grow up with us

It may be one of your children who becomes seriously ill. This is when time becomes finite, when people realise how precious it is. Losing a child to illness or accident is our greatest fear as fathers, and it can happen. It is important to appreciate that their lives, like ours, are finite, and that we therefore need to live our lives understanding that each day may be their last. It is vital not to be morbidly anxious, but you can't help being aware of this every time your children walk out the door.

Once when I was in Washington DC attending a conference, I returned to my hotel room and turned on the TV (which I don't normally do) to get the news. The cameras had just started to pick up the Columbine High School tragedy 'live'. The helicopter was filming, and it was not clear what was going on. I saw children running out of the school and there were reports that there were some children shooting inside. As I was watching, I was desperately hoping that none of the children had been killed in there. When the Sheriff came out and said that 'up to 25 kids had been killed', I could not help starting to cry, as I thought about my own children at school in Australia. When they are young and head off to school or when they are older and start driving cars, you never know if they are going to return. It is crucial to live, within reason, as though today might be either your last day or their last day.

The Emergency Department was extraordinarily busy that afternoon. I helped resuscitate the driver of a car that had collided with a bus. A little girl was killed in the crash. The dead girl's sister had no obvious injuries and her skin sparkled because she was covered in tiny flakes of glass from a shattered window.

Then the girl's father arrived. The family asked would I speak to him. I had no idea what to say, or how I could help, but I couldn't refuse.

I sat him down in the Relatives Room. It was cold. I told him I wished I knew what to say.

And yet I knew that nothing I could say would change anything. I told him that too. He started to talk. Not in terms of graphic descriptions of 'she wasn't breathing, she was dead', but about his little girl. Of the child who had run home from school, delighted with her certificate for winning a swimming race. Of watching her grow up. Of the joy and pride she brought him. I still didn't know what to say. So I said nothing. Then as I stood to leave I realised I was starting to cry.

Letter to the author from a hospital intern, 1999

If we stop taking these things for granted – life, children, time – we will develop a philosophy that enables us to maximise our time with our children. We will be able to stop long enough to see that the sky is very blue and that the trees are very green, and that every day we have on Earth is a gift. We will stop taking time and family for granted.

This approach to life seems to make time slow down, something we all wish would happen. It helps us notice and experience things more deeply. People who understand that their time here is limited are aware of who is important in their lives and of what they should do about that.

Cancer might rob you of that blissful ignorance that once led you to believe that tomorrow stretched forever. In exchange, you are granted the vision to see each today as precious, a gift to be used wisely and richly: no one can take that away. 'Living With Cancer', National Cancer Institute

In his book *How to be your Daughter's Daddy*, Dan Bolin describes how on Halloween 1985 he and his wife took their children, all dressed up in Halloween gear, for a routine medical check-up before going to a party. The routine examination of one of his children showed problems – within hours, it was confirmed that she had leukaemia. He describes the journey of therapy, optimism, pessimism, fear and anxiety, and the ways in which he began to treat every day as a gift, never knowing whether this birthday party would be his daughter's last, if this vacation would be her last. He lists 365 ways to show your daughter that you care. Five years later, Catie died, on another Halloween day.

I learnt a lot from Catie. I hope my other daughter has a better daddy because of what I learnt. There are no perfect daddies. We are all busy, we all say the wrong things and we all struggle trying to know what in the world to do with our kids. Our kids need to know that they are special. This can happen only as they become a priority in our lives. Dan Bolin

When we realise our lives are finite

When I was living in the USA working for Microsoft, my sister was killed in a car accident in Australia. This made me ask myself what it was that I would want to be placed on my tombstone if I died. Would I want it to say, 'He was Vice-President of Microsoft'? I decided that no, I would rather have it say, 'He tried his best as a father and at his work.' However, I didn't want to just go up the coast and grow vegetables, so I had to set out and change my working lifestyle and my schedule so that I could be hopefully a good father and a good employee. Daniel Petre

You only get one shot at it

Getting your time commitments right can't be postponed. A colleague of mine said that for her, parenting was being in a line at the post office. You are on the end of a long queue of people and you have your envelopes and parcels ready and you gradually move forward. When it's your turn you have to do the right thing, because once you've walked out of the post office, you've missed your chance. 'You only get one shot at it,' she says, 'so you can't mess it up' – you can't go back and do it all over again.

I wish I had developed a better relationship with my son. I wish I hadn't worked so hard but had spent more time at home. He hanged himself just outside our house. It kicks you in the guts. I blame myself. His brothers want me to talk about it with them but I just can't. I might try to talk to them about it this Christmas but it is very hard for me. Anonymous, businessman

You can get haunted by the song 'Cat's in the Cradle'. That song is a good lesson for anyone I reckon. You've got to be there for them when they need you most. It doesn't matter how busy your schedule is – it's what you make of it. You only get one go and then the time is gone. You can never get it back again. My brother-in-law used to say, before he passed away, 'Never say "I wish I had" or "why didn't I"'. That sums it up for me. Don't put it off – sometimes I'd come home from football training and the kids would ask me to come out and have a kick. I'd think to myself that this is the last thing I really want to do, but even if I was tired I would do it. You never regret those moments. Michael Malthouse

Some dads make a commitment very early, and if they get bad news, they don't have decisions they regret. In fact just recently I was discussing this with Tony Weller, a 48-year-old schoolteacher who had just months to live. His comments to me are on the opening page of this chapter.

Children's lives are racing by

One of the commonest conversations I have with my friends nowadays is about how fast life seems to move. I remember one old ex-Hollywood star saying that 'she was so old and life was going so fast that it seemed like about every fifteen minutes it was time for the next day's breakfast'. It is great if you can get that sense when the children are young rather than when they are about to leave home and you realise too late what you have missed out on.

When my first daughter was born I was working long hours. One night I came home and Grace was asleep and I said to my wife 'Why isn't Grace up?' She was only a few weeks old and my wife explained that she couldn't just keep her up for my sake. If I wanted to see her she explained that I had to come home earlier. This really shook me up and I then started to make sure I was home (as often as possible) before Grace was put down to sleep.   Daniel Petre

Most of us have choices about how we live our lives

Don't tell yourself, 'I can't do this. I have no choice in the matter.' I think there are three main reasons why fathers work long hours.

1 Real need – sometimes economic and other circumstances make long hours a necessity, if only for a period of time.
2 Self-generated need – if your mortgage and lifestyle have been racked up to generate need, you can convince others that you need to work the long hours you do and you will be right. But how much is real need and how much is self-generated?
3 Subconscious need – whether it is a desire to be the best, to prove yourself to someone, to win, to feel satisfied, etc, these needs, which appropriately drive us at times in our work, can also drive us to overwork.

Although fathers don't really want to work too hard, too many hours, and, given the choice, would choose a rich, happy and fulfilling family life, the very notion of altering work schedules or sacrificing time for children often doesn't cross their radar screens. The pressure and demands of work mean that a lot of fathers simply haven't thought about it as being their choice. Others have, and still struggle with it every day.

I guess my long working hours have always been a difficulty for me in fathering, but it is a choice that I have made and keep making.

Glenn Begley

I would advise young dads to make sure that their full emotional range is available to the children. What do I mean? Well they need to see your joys, your frustrations, and your disappointments, and see how you deal with them. If your career will rob you of that then you need to re-order your career. Lots of people can't do that. I think I am learning more about that all the time. Tim Costello

I know blokes who are as flexible as anything when it comes to fitting in their golf schedule or fishing bug (or their extra-marital affairs, for that matter) who can't find a way of being home for their kids a little more. My suspicion is that they're either locked into a work-is-sacred mindset, or they simply don't know how to be with their own kids and don't even relish the prospect. I see it even in friends, but I don't think I really understand it. Maybe if you delay involvement long enough, if you have no intimacy with them when they're small, then it's too daunting later. Tim Winton

When he's protesting up at Parliament House and the kids ask me why Dad isn't home, I don't make excuses for him – I don't lie and say 'He has no choice.' It's important for kids to realise that Dad has chosen what he does. Therefore I explain that he's made that choice himself and then I explain why he's made that choice.
Jane Cooke

Often we remain passive. We let work rule us, and when it is all over we look back and ask how it happened. Many of my colleagues tell me about the how demanding work is, and how tired they are, but when I ask why they don't change how they work, they tell me they can't.

These comments generate in me a visual image of a runaway bus with them chained to the rear bumper bar, being dragged along, unable to do anything. The truth is that we are mostly not chained to the bumper bar of that bus; we are in the driver's seat, but we just don't take hold of the steering wheel and get control of the bus. We do have a choice, and it is important that we acknowledge that – and that we do make the choice, inevitably, one way or the other.

See work in its true perspective -- get the balance right

The first step towards getting our time commitments right is to escape from the conviction that our work is more important than it ever really is. Work, particularly for busy successful people, always seems more important than it really is. This is particularly the case when we are young. The feelings of insecurity, the need for productivity, the desire to prove ourselves and get established all make work seem much more important at the time than it seems in retrospect.

Many fathers who were interviewed described a feeling of regret about this – they wished they had been able to see their work in its true perspective when they were younger.

If I had my time all over again it most definitely would be a different scenario. I would spend more time at home with kids, especially talking and listening to them.

Robert Vojakovic

If I was talking to a young father today who was moving up the ladder, I would tell him that work is never as important in the long run as it seems to be at the time. The pressure of work makes you feel as though you should keep going, but it is an illusion. I still have not quite got the balance right and it is an ongoing tension in my life. Glenn Begley

Unfortunately my work as a stonemason seemed more important to me than time with the family when I was younger. I guess that was because I felt less financially strong back then. Graham Smith

If I had my time all over again, I'd probably worry less about the job that I do. I think my time commitment to the kids has been okay, but I would probably try to focus more on the kids, to disengage more from work. I don't give myself an A+ on this one, I'm afraid. John Anderson

Another piece of advice for young dads is to always keep your job in context. There is tendency in all of us to think our job is the centre of the universe. For example, once when I was a league coach and we lost a game I couldn't sleep that night. I got up at 3 o'clock in the morning and went walking around in the rain thinking. Suddenly I realised something. No-one in China cares that my team lost today. In fact no-one in Adelaide even cares. It's not really all that important. All you can do is give it your best shot, and if it doesn't work you don't need to implode. It's the same for your job. You need to see it in its real context. Dennis Cometti

My advice to a young politician would be not to get carried away. Canberra really goes to your head, and you can become isolated and lonely, and it's

easy to go off the rails. There is a high divorce rate. I would also recommend that young men be careful of their time commitment, because in politics most of your life is lived outside the family. Basically, if you are under 40, don't do it. I was 32, and that was too young. Kim Beazley

The corporate world is full of bullshit. It's a means to an end, not an end in itself. The real end is what you do in life with your family, your kids, your friends, etc – it's outside of work, not inside of work, that your real achievements are measured. Warren Reynolds

I have a job that people think of as creative. But is there anything more creative than being a parent? Or anything more important? My readers might evaporate. My reputation will likely fade. But maybe my kids will remember our times together. Maybe the better things I did will inspire little things in them, things that might be passed on to their kids. A few fart jokes at least. As a parent, you're like the butterfly wings flapping in the Amazon that cause a typhoon in the South China Sea. You don't know what an influence you'll have. It's your best chance to do good. Given the choice, I'd rather be a mediocre writer and remembered by my kids as a decent sort of father. Tim Winton

Sometimes work opportunities that seem great present themselves, though in retrospect we sometimes wish we had waited a bit longer.

The hardest time for us was when our children were quite young and I was Treasurer. One year was particularly hard and I look back on that and realise how very understanding my wife was. It is a demanding portfolio, and the kids were young. I question whether my timing was good on that one, accepting that portfolio at that time. It was hard. John Howard

If I had my time all over again I would have voted for Sir McFarlane Burnet to be twelve years younger so that I wouldn't have become Director of the Walter Eliza Hall Institute at the age of 30. It's really hard to take on a leadership [position] when your kids are young. My life became fragmented and diversified with committees, fundraising, etc, and it became quite easy for this to invade the rest of my life. My advice to young people is to postpone success to a stage of life when you're more personally fulfilled in other parts of your life. Gus Nossal

Too much focus on the family

Finally, a warning: remember, there is another side to the bell curve – you can commit too much time to family. You may have met families like this. The parents never do anything but spend time with the kids. Children have priority in any conversation.

Parents need to get a life, to work on their own relationship, to maintain their own friends, or they risk becoming introverted. And they will model that for their children, so that the kids too may have difficulty forming relationships.

Kids don't need their parents to be always focused on them. It puts too much pressure on them. These parents need to get a life of their own, get interesting lives, have good friends. Then their kids will see that their parents are interesting, their lives are meaningful and they know how to have fun. If they don't, it puts too much pressure on the kids, because they are their parents' only measurement of success in life.   Stephen Harvey

What worries me a little bit about your writing a book like this, Bruce, is that some blokes will start spending so much time with their kids that they won't look after themselves. Don't let men become so obsessed with focusing on their kids that they don't keep up their own friendships, activities and personal development. Kids have to learn to respect the needs of parents and you need to model the fact that parents are individuals, too. This helps the kids to learn boundaries. It tells the kids, 'Hey, I am a human being, too.'   Jacqui Robinson

Some dads have found that spending all their time with the kids can reduce their own friendship networks.

I guess in some ways our family is a bit of a closed unit, which is a bit like the way my dad behaved, although I'm not sure if that is relevant. We are repeating that pattern a bit, too. Being so available to my children has definitely reduced my time for friendships with other people.

Geoff Creelman

Spending *all* of your time with your children is not always better.

This point is illustrated in the following figure: The 'My family has become my whole life' bell curve.

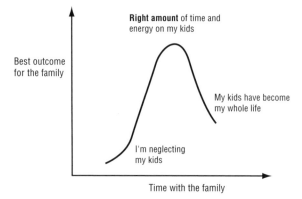

QUESTIONS

- Do you take time with your children for granted?
- Do you really have a choice about how you organise your time?
- Who is stopping you from making your children more of a priority?
- What is the worst thing that could happen if you sacrificed a bit to give them more time?
- Have you fallen into the trap of thinking your work is more important to you than it really should be?
- How susceptible are you to peer pressure to overwork?

Not letting good intentions fade

It is important to realise that what books can achieve is limited. Books tend to influence a lot of people a little bit and a small number of people dramatically. Why is this? The answer is simple – reading the written word tends to have a short-term effect because the reader doesn't put what is read into practice. This is clearly true in a number of areas, for example in diets and management techniques. Books and magazine articles regularly come up with new diets, and overweight people regularly read them. It has been said that if the person who reads about a new diet each month just stuck to the first one they ever read, they wouldn't be overweight – it's not the early motivation that's the problem, it's staying on track with it.

Similarly, bookshops are full of books on how to manage a business well. The same problem exists here. The core elements of all these books are largely the same; the main attraction to a reader is often simply that they are new. If the reader had done what it said to do in the first book, they'd probably find that they were more successful in managing their business.

Initial enthusiasm is a good start ...

I think if dads go to the birth of their child then that softening starts there. This has really only been done in the last generation, and I think watching the birth of the child and then holding the little baby is the start of a father being a better dad.   Seamus Doherty

Some of my happiest moments have been when the children were born. When my first son, Jonathan was born, I rode my bike over from the hospital and apparently rode through the sprinklers and came in soaking wet. I just felt like shouting out to the whole world, 'Hey everyone, I'm a dad! I'm a dad!' It was the same with Ryan. Joel's birth was very special, too. They were all wonderful. Matthew, however, I collected when he was adopted, and that was a very special time of a different kind.   Glenn Begley

It was wonderful holding them as babies and knowing that they were my children.   Paul Bannan

I have read books on fathering but it's really putting it into action every day that's the hardest thing.   Tim Costello

A parenting course made me ask, 'Is there an alternative way of fathering?' It didn't happen immediately, though, but in time I started to change. I wish I could change straight away, but old habits die hard, and I had to make a conscious effort every day to use what I'd learnt.   Peter de Blanc

... but good fathering requires ongoing hard work.

A burst of fatherly enthusiasm followed by a void is unlikely to be helpful. In some ways it could be a hindrance. Just as a swimming pool does not look after itself once it is built, but needs ongoing maintenance, so does fathering. No amount of initial enthusiasm about improved fathering will work if there is not a strategy for maintaining it. This point is illustrated in the following figure:

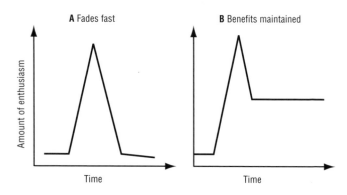

Reality checks are okay, and some people do respond, but I think it doesn't last more than a few weeks because men get sucked in by work again. It's insidious, like cancer. What they won't 'admit to themselves is that work feels better, that people respond to them better [there], and that there are more rewards. When men first change their lifestyle and start spending more time at home they often feel like they're not really needed. That's not surprising because the family has learnt to cope without them. Initially no-one gives a shit but after a while dad becomes part of the family lifestyle and he starts to be needed. They have to stick with it, see how the home front works and break through that barrier. It's easier if men start this early, bonding with their children enough to become a necessary part of their life.

Daniel Petre

It can be hard to stay on track with fathering. It usually requires encouragement and support from like-minded individuals. This support can be hard for some men to find. Indeed, men in modern Western societies are often isolated and lonely, with few true friends with whom they can discuss issues close to the heart. This is made worse by divorce, because the male reliance on women for social interactions combined with a 30–40 percent divorce rate can leave a lot of men without any close relationships at all. Also, the inherent competitiveness of men can spill over into relationships, leading to a fear of disclosing problems in the family or even simply concerns about how well you are fathering.

To stay on track as dads we need the wisdom of others, especially other men. I've met with three other blokes for breakfast most Fridays for over ten years now and we all really value those times to talk and off-load. I only wish I had more of that. I also appreciate a handful of close mates who I try to catch up with regularly.   Tim Costello

On a more personal, day-to-day level, the best thing you can do as a dad is hang around with other dads, and talk about what to do. You can salvage all kinds of wisdom and ideas, since everyone has different and worthwhile approaches. I think the biggest message of the men's movement may be this enormous sense of relief, that what we were trying to be – heroic lone battlers against a cold, hard world – is impossible and we may as well stop. It's to find brotherhood and sisterhood and be human, and this is an actual strength and resilience that comes from our weakness and limitations. Drop the superman delusion. Accept your real limitations. You can't have it all, you can't do it all, so what are you going to choose and value? Work with modest and humble goals, so you are free to live and love.   Steve Biddulph

I do start to take the kids for granted from time to time and drift off a bit. What pulls me into line I suppose is my love for the kids and my desire to succeed as a father. Sometimes it is Cherith who reminds me of things I should be doing. We also have close friends with whom we talk about our parenting and what we are all doing. We encourage each other in it. We try to stay positive in our discussions with other parents about our kids. We try not to describe our kids in negative terms like 'he is a little ...' or 'she is driving me ... ' but instead take the view that the kids are a gift from God to be enjoyed.   Patrick Gangemi

Attending the kids' birth is a good start, but is only the very first step. Dads have to then stick with it. I've been a health representative and had to go round building sites and three fathers that I know of have just walked into the bush and killed themselves when they couldn't accept the failure of their family. Two hung themselves and one put a bullet in his head. It really requires a lot of commitment and you have to get in early.   Mick Bolton

Summary

■ A certain amount of anxiety for the children is helpful – it stops us taking our time with them for granted; but too much anxiety for them is unhelpful, for them and for us.

■ There are no guarantees that we will live to see our children grow up – or that they will live to adulthood – so seize the opportunity to spend time with them now.

■ Reality checks, like the death of a friend, help remind us of the preciousness of time.

■ Don't be fooled into saying you have no choice in how you spend your time.

■ Excessive focus on the family, to the exclusion of friends, adult lifestyle and work can be counterproductive for them and for you.

■ It is not enough to read a book like this. You need to work at maintaining the enthusiasm and energy – otherwise they will fade. Re-read fathering books each year.

■ Set up your own reminder system for fathering activities that you've planned – via a diary, computer calender prompts, whatever works for you.

 IDEAS FOR ACTION:

Here are a few suggestions for how to stay on track with fathering.

(a) Keep a diary and enter the things that you plan to do each week.

(b) Find two other fathers who have read this book or who you think might be open to the things discussed in it. Lend them your copy or buy them a copy as a gift.

(c) Arrange to meet with them in a month's time to talk about it.

(d) Keep each other on track. Each month choose a section to read and telephone each other or meet over coffee to ask how well you've done in that area.

(e) Get together to do some of the things suggested in the book – take your children out camping together, for instance. It's easier to keep doing things when there is a group doing them with you.

(f) Regularly log into the fathering websites described in the Resources section, and subscribe to those websites that send you regular emails reminding you of some of the things that you can do.

(g) Discuss your plans with your partner, if you are in a relationship. Make a written list of agreed, goals together and check on them together regularly.

(h) Make a note in your diary to re-read this and other books annually in order to regularly restimulate your ideas.

(i) Subscribe to a fathering magazine.

(j) Set up reminders in your computer calendar to do specific fathering activities that you've decided to try.

WHAT ?!? You want to borrow my car?
Who are you? George? George who?
Oh. Right ... Um... Ask your mum !

Notes

This is a brief list of references. More detailed lists of relevant publications can be obtained from many of the websites listed in the Resources section.

Page 3 Being a good father does... Andrews, Judy A., Hops, Hyman, Duncan, Susan C., 'Adolescent modeling of parent substance use: The moderating effect of the relationship with the parent.' *J Family Psych*, 997; 11: 259–270. See also the following:
Popenoe, D., *Life without father*. The Free Press, New York, 1996.
Lamb, M., *The Role of the Father in Child Development*, Wiley, New York, 1996.
Fathers' involvement in their children's schools, National Center for Educational Statistics. Washington D.C., GPO, 1997.
Page 3 The accused boy... Judge Antoinette Kennedy, sentencing a twenty-year-old father to gaol. *The West Australian*. 21/12/2000, p. 12.
Page 16 Because where there are two parents... Hardy, J.B., Shapiro, S., Mellits, E.D., Skinner, E.A., Astone N.M., Ensminger, M., LaVeist, T., Baumgardner, R.A., Starfield, B.H., 'Self-sufficiency at ages 27 to 33 years: factors present between birth and 18 years that predict educational attainment among children born to inner-city families.' *Pediatrics*. 1997; 99: pp. 80–7.
Page 16 This description is adapted... There are numerous references to the work of Abraham Maslow. A google.com Internet search generated 8 800 findings. I recommend *Toward a Psychology of Being*, 3rd ed., Wiley, New York, 1998.
Page 17 This has been well described... Plunkett, M.C., Southall, D.P., 'War and children', *Archives of Disease in Childhood*, 1998; 78: pp. 72–7.
Page 34 Evidence from... http://www.wel.org.au/announce/denoon/99mlake.htm
Page 34 Research shows... (box) Melissa Stevens, *The West Australian*, 12/7/2000.
Page 37 One quarter of... http://www.familyone.wa.gov.au/facts.asp
Pages 37–38 For example 63 percent... US DHHS Bureau of Census, US Dept of Justice Special Report 1988, National Institutes of Mental Research, 4th Annual Research Roundtable. June 19, 2000, Washington, D.C. http://www.nimh.nih.gov/research/roundtable.cfm
Page 36 Fatherlessness is... (Jenny Shipley quote) http://www.scoop.co.nz/stories/PA9910/ S00245.htm

Page 73 My father would... (Donald Bradman quote) ABC Online News, 2001. Australian Broadcasting Corporation, 26/2/01.

Page 91 That approach has... Cromie, W.J., 'Death Rate from Heart Disease Falls', *http://www.news.harvard.edu/science/archives/medicine/heart_20.Feb.97.html*

Page 102 ... Fathers who are confident... *http://www.tameside.gov.uk/edugen/eydp/documents/familyfriendly.pdf*; Jain, A., et. al., 'Beyond fathering behaviour – Types of dads', *J Fam Psych* 1996; 10: pp. 431–442.

Page 107 As a radio interviewer... and *My children have given me...* Liam is a lawyer and ABC radio interviewer. *Perth Weekly*. vol 3–33, 30/8/2000.

Page 113 The evidence shows that... There are a lot of references relevant to this issue. One example is Walker, L.O., Fleschler, R.G., Heaman, M., 'Is a healthy lifestyle related to stress, parenting confidence, and health symptoms among new fathers?', *Can J of Nursing Res.*, 1998; 30: pp. 21–3.

Page 113 Play is more than just... Hansel, T., *When I Relax I Feel Guilty*, David C Cook, Elgin, Il. 1979.

Page 168 The message is... (Peter Richie quote) *Business Review Weekly*. 22/10/99.

Page 172 In those days... Shaklee, H., *Fathers in America: 100 Years of Change*, University of Idaho Cooperative Extension. *http://www.ets.uidaho.edu/CCC/CCC%20Families/Research/fathers.htm*

Page 174 It was so commonplace... Jesus at 12 years of age. Luke 2: 41–50.

Page 176 A lot has been written... The Generation X Coalition, *http://members.aol.com/genXcoal/genXcoal.htm*

Page 203 Don't expect to know... (M. Scott Peck quote) *Further Along the Road less Travelled*. Vol. 2., Simon & Schuster Audio New York, 1993.

Page 215 My best advice for dads... (Peter Chappell quote) Ephesians 6:4.

Page 217 During the Columbine High School massacre... *Time Magazine*, cover story, 3/5/99.

Page 217 Rebecca said... (Rebecca Crew quote) *The Post Newspaper*, 18/11/2000, p. 16.

Page 220 I learnt a lot from Catie... (Dan Bolin quote) Bolin, D., *How to be your Daughter's Daddy: 365 ways to show her you care*, Pinon Press, Colorado Springs, 1993.

Acknowledgements

I am grateful to all those men, women and children who allowed me to interview them and who shared some of their most personal thoughts and experiences with me. I hope that any young father who reads this book and learns from your wisdom feels something of the same gratitude towards you that I feel.

I especially wish to thank the Beale and Weller families for allowing me into their private world of grief to take what their fathers/husbands had to say and share it with other men.

Thanks to Maree Branigan and Ann Jolghazi for typing parts of the manuscript and to my friends and family for reviewing parts of the book for me at times.

Thanks to Rex, Sean and the team at Finch Publishing – it sure is complicated writing a book like this!

Finally, ultimate thanks to my wonderful family – Jacqui, Simon, Scott and Amy – for without them this book would have little substance, energy or meaning, just like the rest of my life.

Resources

Only websites are listed below. Lists of fathering books and organisations can be readily found on most of these sites. Not all the relevant sites are listed; a more extensive list is available at http://www.brucerobinson.com.au.

Australasian
http://www.parentingideas.com.au/
http://law.gov.au/aghome/commaff/lafs/frsp/mensforum/Welcome.html
http://www.manhood.com.au
http://www.fatherandchild.org.nz

North American
http://www.fathersworld.com/
http://www.asanet.org/Sections/Family/links.htm
http://family.go.com/raisingkids/
http://www.fatherhood.org/
http://www.family.org/
http://www.fathers.com/
http://www.daddyshome.com/
http://fatherwork.byu.edu/
http://www.fathering.org/
http://directory.google.com/Top/Home/Family/Parenting/Fathering/
http://themenscenter.com/NMR12.htm
http://www.vix.com/pub/men/nofather/nodad.html#dad
http://fatherhood.hhs.gov/CFSForum/front.htm
http://dadstoday.com/
http://fatherhood.about.com/parenting/fatherhood/
http://www.fathersfirst.org
http://www.cyfc.umn.edu/fathernet/
http://www.dadsworld.com/
http://www.family-friendly-fun.com/
http://www.parenthoodweb.com/
http://www.parenthoodweb.com/
http://www.researchforum.org/

Fathering magazine sites
http://www.fathermag.com/
http://www.dadmag.com/
http://www.fathersdirect.com/news/

Other Finch titles

ParentCraft
*A practical guide to
raising children well
(2nd edition)*
Ken and Elizabeth
Mellor
ISBN 187645119X

**The Myth of Male
Power**
*Why men are the
disposable sex*
Warren Farrell
ISBN 1876451300

Raising boys
*Why boys are different
– and how to help
them become happy
and well-balanced men*
Steve Biddulph
ISBN 0646314181

**Women Can't Hear
What Men Don't Say**
*Destroying the myths,
creating love*
Warren Farrell
ISBN 1876451319

Manhood
*An action plan for
changing men's lives*
Steve Biddulph
ISBN 0646261444

**Father and Child
Reunion**
*How to bring the dads
we need to the
children we love*
Warren Farrell
ISBN 1876451327

Stories of Manhood
*Journeys into the
hidden hearts of men*
Steve Biddulph
ISBN 1876451106

Dealing with Anger
*Self-help solutions for
men*
Frank Donovan
ISBN 187645105X

On Their Own
*Boys growing up
underfathered*
Rex McCann
ISBN 1876451092

Fathers After Divorce
*Building a new life
and becoming a
successful separated
parent*
Michael Green
ISBN 1876451009

Life Smart
*Choices for young
people about
friendship, family
and future*
Vicki Bennett
ISBN 1876451130

Other Finch titles

The Happy Family
Ken and Elizabeth Mellor
ISBN 1876451122

Easy Parenting
Ken and Elizabeth Mellor
ISBN 1876451114

Fear-free children
Dr Janet Hall
ISBN 1876451238

Fight-free Families
Dr Janet Hall
ISBN 187645122X

Kids Food Health 1
Nutrition and your child's development – the first year
Dr Patricia McVeagh & Eve Reed
ISBN 1876451149

Kids Food Health 2
Nutrition and your child's development – from toddler to preschooler
Dr Patricia McVeagh & Eve Reed
ISBN 1876451157

Kids Food Health 3
Nutrition and your child's development – from school-age to teenage
Dr Patricia McVeagh & Eve Reed
ISBN 1876451165

Motherhood
Making it work for you
Jo Lamble and Sue Morris
ISBN 1876451033

Online and Personal
The reality of internet relationships
Jo Lamble and Sue Morris
ISBN 1876451173

Side by Side
How to think differently about your relationship
Jo Lamble and Sue Morris
ISBN 1876451092

Chasing Ideas
The fun of freeing your child's imagination
Christine Durham
ISBN 1876451181

Boys in Schools
Addressing the real issues – behaviour, values and relationships
Rollo Browne and Richard Fletcher
ISBN 0646239589

Fathers, Sons and Lovers
Men talk about their lives from 1930s to today
Dr Peter West
ISBN 0646288164

Bullybusting
How to help children deal with teasing and bullying
Evelyn Field
ISBN 1876451041

Girls' Talk
Young women speak their hearts and minds
Maria Palotta-Chiarolli
ISBN 1876451025

Index